LONG GOING

LONG GOING

Sophie Calon

HONNO MEMOIR

First published in Great Britain in 2025 by Honno Press
D41, Hugh Owen Building, Aberystwyth University, Ceredigion, SY23 3DY

1 2 3 4 5 6 7 8 9 10

Copyright © Sophie Calon 2025
Photographs © Sophie Calon 2025

The right of Sophie Calon to be identified as the Author of the Work has been asserted in accordance with the Copyright, Designs and Patents Act 1988.
All rights reserved.

This book is a memoir, reflecting the author's recollection of events over time. Some names and identifying characteristics of individuals have been changed to protect their privacy.

No part of the book may be reproduced, stored in a retrieval system, or transmitted in any form, or by any means, electronic, mechanical, photocopying, recording or otherwise without the prior permission of the copyright owner.

A catalogue record for this book is available from the British Library.

Published with the financial support of the Books Council of Wales.

9781916821248
9781916821255 (ebook)

Cover design by Ifan Bates
Typeset by Elaine Sharples
Printed by 4edge Ltd

for Bee

I
1993–2019

bounce back

There was a dad with me once.

He drifted slowly, unsteady on his feet. I yearned for closure eventually. Truth is, I grieved his going before learning he had gone. Not a surprise, that news, but still a shock when it lit my phone screen. Those pixels stung like citrus on a cut.

People often speak of *hiraeth*. Untranslatable, they say. Is it? Split it in two, *hir|aeth*, and you get long|gone. And that's the crux of it, if you ask me. A longing for someone, something, sometime, someplace long gone. A heave in the gut for the no longer reachable.

Where we truly lack the words is a more searing sensation: the longing for what's fading just beyond reach. Within sight, between here and gone, like ink greying in cold sunlight. *Hir|mynd*, long|going.

My dad's long going was dark and frightening. Tiring, too. All that not knowing if, when he did come back, he might stick around this time. In Welsh, there's no word for 'have'. Someone or something is either with us or not with us. No possession, only presence.

Yes, there was a dad with me once.

I last heard from him two years, seven months, and twenty-five days before his death. An email to tell me of his own dad's death. I sent a curt, kind reply, then let my dad have the last word:

Grandad

Thu 2 May 2019 1:34 PM

I'm in Barry at the moment. It's all very sad. The conversations are about Death Certificates, the funeral, undertakers etc. I'm finding it all really tough.
Anyway, I'm determined to bounce back and I am doing everything I can to achieve that. Keep up the reading. I have been doing more of that than for some time (and getting beyond page 6). It's been a great help recently. Love you.

Why didn't I write back after that? Fatigue, I guess. There was too much pretence in things we said to each other. For instance, his line about doing everything he can. It felt like a lie. To himself, I suspect, as well as to me. He might have kidded himself into thinking he meant it. Bottom line, it was false, but it wasn't his fault. I kind of get that now. *Gwin*, wine. Red, mainly. Could you tell? Stains like hell. Splattered across us all, his collateral.

As for how to get him bouncing back, well, I was at a loss. Might I have done more? At first I didn't know if I should, then I didn't know if I could. My efforts felt belated. By then his drinking had asserted itself centre stage, spotlit and erratic. The show went on, and on, and grotesquely on. The more I grew up, the more he crumpled. I'm told I shouldn't, but even so I worry it was cause and effect. My growing up, his tumbling down. He raised me to live with joy, curiosity, confidence, while he tipped slowly into oblivion. Obliterating all that possible living.

As a child, I believed every word my dad said. He was the wisest of men, I thought. I trusted him more than anyone. Now I'm a year older than he was when my birth made him a dad aged twenty-seven. I like to think, if it had panned out differently, if he hadn't died twenty-eight years later outside a Volkswagen dealership one night, that we'd still be good mates. I don't know if I wish he were still here. It haunted me, that shadowy figure he was towards the end. I do wish, though, that I'd had more time to gather some wisdom of my own, anything that might have done something.

It's confusing to love someone who's dying from what might look like an opt-in terminal illness. And how do you square the fact that its key symptom, heavy drinking, is so socially acceptable? Let's face it, mandated at times. Then, at some point, somehow, fatal. I assumed the end was fixed, maybe before it was so. I couldn't bear his long going, so I went myself. I fear my absence had a role in making it certain.

I'm still figuring it out. There's no easy cure for this, no medicine over the counter. By the time I had seen what other people's lives looked like, that is, by the time I was better equipped, it felt like he was already beyond reach.

Oblivion for him, vivid for us. We were told to forgive it all along the way, to forget until the next time the next time the next time. Let bygones be bygones. Long gone, now. But what about this long going, is that worth remembering? I think so.

∼

Where to start?

I could tell you about my dad's change of setting. Act I: three kids, married, close-knit family home. Sought-after neighbourhood. Equity partnership, no less, in a top Welsh law firm. Act II: mostly solo missions, prison cells, homeless shelters. Underpasses, sometimes. Leaking tents in the bushes off Hope Street, worse times. Hope, the thing that weathered.

I could tell you about his change of habits. Act I: painting canvases on Saturday mornings, running marathons. Act II: roaming the city's gutters, brawling with other addicts.

I could tell you about the way he treated people, though this is murkier in terms of *earlier/later*. He made us laugh a lot, even beyond the end. He could be hilarious, generous, contagiously courageous. Rude, consistently, to those he didn't respect. More and more, he made us cry, lashing out, aggrieved at the betrayals he perceived in us reaching our limits with him.

To my sister Bee's partner, Lloyd, our dad was The Wanderer. It suited him, this. Intrepid, free-spirited. He used to quote *Ice Age*, a film my brother Danny and he knew almost by heart.

'Are you ready for adventure?'

'Yes, sir!'

'For danger?'

'Yes, sir!'

'For death?'

'Uhh, can you repeat the question?'

My dad wasn't ready for death. Who is at fifty-five? He wilfully swerved lawyers' advice to make a will. To them, he was deteriorating. To him, he was invincible. Invincible!

~

The moment I hear he's gone, *gone* gone, it's grief and it's relief, indistinguishable, truly untranslatable to the daughter I once was to him, the one who'd follow him anywhere. Up a skeletal gorge, into lightning-striking sea, through howling dunes, all the while whistling a happy tune.

The news comes while I'm at the Robin Hood pub. Just uphill from Hebden Bridge, West Yorkshire. 27 December 2021. My partner, Ash, and I moved here a year ago. We're a good two hours northeast of Sherwood Forest, but it's the vibe of the thing. Men here likewise took from the rich and gave to the poor. We leave coppers on the local hero's grave in Heptonstall as a mark of respect. Pity how it all ended. Violence, betrayals, sudden death. I see resemblances.

It's dusk. The pub's toasty, all steamed-up glass and flushed cheeks. The smoky open fire crackles and splutters amber sparks. Christmas is still in our hearts. For the first time in years, the valley could gather merrily together.

We're tucked in, my friends and I, at the round table by the door. I insisted they took the cushioned bench and am perched on a stool, rickety on the flagstones. I play with the beer mats while we chat. Elva, the landlady, shuffles past us to the bar, where beer is three quid a pint. Me, I'm midway through a medium house red. I regret this only in hindsight.

For now I've slipped my phone from my pocket to show off a photo of recent valley fog. You'd think it was the ocean, a pale expanse floating around the clifftops. Except I've stopped, gone AWOL mid-sentence. Staring, chest clenched, clutching a few seconds to digest this.

In my palm is a different sort of mist, a daze of missed calls and texts. At the top, just minutes back, the latest from my best friend:

Call me when you see this.

I should speak but I can't quite breathe. There's no mistaking what these words mean.

'Just need to—', I mutter to the ground as I leave.

Outside the air is dingy and the hills shiver. There is no one out here. The faded awning is folded away. I call Lisa. It's twenty-four years since our first day of school. Two or three years, maybe, since I first sensed she'd be the one to tell me this. Intuition, call it what you like. It tends to be right.

She picks up straightaway. My hands are cold and clammy.

'Li?'

'Are you with people?'

'Yeah, Em and her sister.'

'It's your dad—'

'He's died, hasn't he.' I say it fast, flat. It's not a question. I say it so she doesn't have to.

'Yes.' Her voice breaks. 'I'm so sorry. I'm so sorry.'

Fog and clarity collide, the weight of this ending and the end of this waiting. I tip backwards onto a bench and sit silently. The trees lower their eyes and shake their bare heads forlornly. The call is short.

I duck back into the pub. The pub, of all places. That scares me. My friends look at my face and rise. They've guessed. After all, it was only a matter of time.

'We should probably head off,' I mutter, fumbling with my coat and jacket. In my head, my dad's voice echoes, echoes. ('Whose *côt*'s that *siaced*?')

I'm tangling the fabrics, snagging the wrists. Elva, the landlady, takes my arm, draws apart the sleeves, and drapes the layers over me.

'It's my dad,' I say, as if that explains it.

'Do you have far to go?' she asks with gentle eyes.

'Just down the lane,' I smile, my face sluiced with soundless tears.

Behind her, that half-full glass of mine sits expectant on its mat. I turn away, flustered. As we walk, my thoughts meander aloud. More questions that aren't questions. I try to assemble normality.

'I'll have to go to Cardiff, will I? I mean, who'd plan the funeral, it has to be me, no one else will.'

Frost is edging across the soft mossy walls. The sun has gone now, eclipsed by our steep slopes. No breeze, for a change, but a chill in the stillness. We pass the green clock where it's always twenty-six minutes to four. The hands went quiet a long while ago.

'You don't have to do anything,' my friends reply, incorrectly.

Ten minutes later, it's dark when we say bye at their car. I apologise for the gloomy end to their visit. They tell me not to be silly. I am sorry, though. I wish them a safe drive then walk towards my home, where Ash has flicked on the front light ahead of my return.

'Hellooo,' he sings as I turn the key in the lock.

He's reading on the sofa, our kittens dozing beside him. The lamp glows with warm tones. Soft notes murmur from the vinyl on our antique cabinet. I don't want to shatter it, this beautiful life I've tried so hard to earn all these years. I pause and linger on the step ahead of what I have to say next, the first of many times.

'My dad has died.'

Ash is open-mouthed, stunned silent. One of the baby cats rolls over, big stretch. Big yawn. I turn to close the front door.

what's it all about

There's a comfort now in reaching back, back to the longest gone, now that the long going is over. Back to before my dad's drinking took over our lives. I can't say before his drinking. That existed before I did, I'm told.

I regularly replay scenes from life in my head, embedding their details. I tuck the scripts into the corners for safe-keeping. It reassures me, having a grasp of who said or did what, when, where. A sense of order, of sorts.

'Have I ever told you,' my dad often told me, 'that you won first prize in the lottery of life?'

In a dusty poly pocket he kept a copy of *The Times* bought at Heath Hospital on the day of my birth in 1993. 'Dreams can come true,' Gabrielle sang over and over that summer. That line was bang on, my dad said.

A year and a half later, my brother Danny came along. This was less dreamy. Skin as blue as the January Monday that spewed him out, he survived through a fortunate shift change and an emergency blood transfusion after a fresh midwife took one look at him and barked, 'Get this baby to NICU now.'

'Ye gods,' midwives whispered to each other, 'Don't fancy that poor dab's chances.' They didn't clock the floppy-haired guy as the father. My dad heard every ominous word as they passed him in the corridor.

The intensive care staff took photos, in case we needed them to remember Danny by. Yet fate saw to it that there were albums, plural, stuffed with silliness and wide grins. Getting a copy of *The Times* slipped my dad's mind this time. Understandable, that.

I have memories from when I was two, three. Unusual, I do realise. Moments like when our nursery group trundled to the local allotments in the sunshine. Like when I met my first teacher, how I peeked out from beneath my dad's suit jacket as he cradled me in Mrs Bennett's technicolour classroom. Like when I twirled into our conservatory during a party and froze on seeing him smoking with his mates. He hid the cigarette behind his back a second too late.

There were so many parties. Our home swayed with laughter and 90s pop. *Livin' La Vida Loca. Viva Forever.* Glasses sloshed abundantly, topped up as they went along. People streamed in from all over the neighbourhood. The door was always open. I was proud to be my parents' daughter. They were cool and young. They made the fun.

Abruptly, in April 1999, life was not so fun for a while. My mum, nine months pregnant with Bee, lost her dad to motor neurone disease. I cried, held tight by my dad, when he told me the news. A few weeks later, I thought Danny was gone too. He had been plodding along okay. That changed on 27 April 1999.

My dad made me get it all out, to process it, whether or not he did so himself. We sat by our huge desktop computer and he typed what I said aloud. I was five and Danny was four. It was that bit of each year when he almost caught up with me.

25 April 1999

I am a little girl. My name is Sophie. I live in a house with Mummy and Daddy and my brother Danny. I love my world ...

27 April 1999

... I went in the bath with Danny. Mummy was hanging the washing on the line and Grandma was in the kitchen when I shouted that Danny was making a funny noise. He was making a rumbling sound and he was splashing with his feet. Then he seemed to go to sleep. Grandma ran upstairs. Grandma shouted to Mummy. Then she ran upstairs too. Grandma phoned for the ambulance which came very quickly. Grandma had to look after me because Mummy went with Danny in the ambulance. I thought he was dead but he wasn't. Nan and Grandad came to our house and so did Lizzy, Aunty Meryl, and Uncle Glyn. I was reading my book.

I remember these things clearly, perhaps thanks to my dad tweezing them out of me. It was a Tuesday evening. Our mum normally wouldn't have left us alone in the bath. She had been coaxed down by her mum, over ours for her aperitif.

'Good grief, they'll be fine,' Grandma had said, awaiting her glass of Spar's bottom-shelf Chardonnay.

Even in mourning Grandma looked immaculate, her short blonde curls clipped back, her hawk-like green-grey eyes underlined in thick black kohl. Chunky necklaces, loose layers of *brocante*-bartered clothing. She took pride in her appearance, a legacy of her childhood in the Rhondda and the beauty contests she had won. We were forbidden from calling her Grandma to her face.

'*Annie*,' she glared. 'I'm far too young to be a grandmother.'

That evening, it wasn't long before I shouted down to them. My mum ran in and hauled Danny's wet, taut body onto the floorboards. She bent over him, her stomach bulging. He was unconscious, juddering.

'Danny, talk to me, Danny you want tea? Juice? Lemonade? Coffee?—'

Danny doesn't drink coffee, I thought. The narrow room, just a bath and sink, grew dimmer with every minute he didn't wake up. My teeth began chattering while I sat in the water, by now cold and shallower without my brother. With rising desperation, our mum started wailing.

'Talk to me, Danny, talk to me talk to me—'

Those words echo, echo in my head sometimes. 'Talk to me talk to me talk to me.'

There's something altering about white water. A shift so quick it traps air and froths, like Danny did in the '99 storm that hit our bathtub. That shift, so quick, and with it we could never quite rest again.

I thought he was dead but he wasn't.

From then, Danny's seizures kept us eternally, infernally jumpy. They struck at any moment, no warning. He fell unconscious and shook for minutes that felt like days. We placed him on his side and said things like, 'It's alright, we're here. Everything's okay.'

I don't know if he heard us. Then, just as abruptly, he went still, slept, and woke with a headache. If he didn't come out of the seizure, we rang 999. In those early years, it could be a long time before he returned to us.

Grand mal, this type of seizure used to be called. *Great evil.* Now they're known as tonic–clonic. Something to do with the muscle activity. Danny had to wear a padded blue helmet around school to prevent his head from smacking the ground. I felt something in my stomach each time he walked into our assembly. A stab of protectiveness, a gurgle of worry for my brittle brother.

As Danny got older, the fits got subtler. At times he simply tensed, unconscious but staring with a grin. We watched his eyes, looking for signs that he wasn't with us. In ten years' time, it would be our dad's eyes that we'd watch for signs of absence. I think the two were linked.

Every seizure snapped neurons in Danny's brain. His progress ground nearly to a halt. He was two school years below me, but he dropped further and further behind. This broke my dad's heart. Once I was playing with his office Dictaphone and found an old recording of a child singing *Twinkle, Twinkle, Little Star* sweetly, at ease.

'*Who* is that?' I squeaked.

'It was your brother,' my dad said. I heard a sadness in his voice at how Danny had regressed.

My mum went into labour two weeks after that first seizure. Again, my dad was too preoccupied to buy *The Times*. He took me and Danny to a local fête that bright Saturday morning. Early May, four years AD (anno Danny). I ate a Welsh cake and my dad bought us a badminton set. The baby still hadn't arrived by the afternoon. I detailed all this in *Sophie's Memoirs*, still a work-in-progress then.

Daddy said the baby was a slowcoach.

Danny and I would have to sleep at Grandma's house, two miles southwest. We trooped over by foot with our dad. On the way, I found a flower from a conker tree and put it in the bag with our pyjamas. No one was in when we arrived. We played outside with our new set until Danny flung the shuttlecock into Grandma's tall, prim hedge.

The baby still hadn't come by the time we went to bed, but later Grandma woke me up to say my sister had been born. I wanted to go straight to the Heath to see her, but I was told I had to wait until the morning. The next day I updated *Sophie's Memoirs*:

I love her. She is cute.

~

The noughties boomed in, heady with dial-up and scented gel pens and ponchos and new ringtones to select. We were green, carefree, and (in)famous among our suburbs.

Childhood took place within half a mile. Cyncoed, Cardiff, Wales. Nursery, primary school, and high school were all just a quick walk through Nant Fawr Woods. Our world was intimate. We lived simply, rooted to our routines.

Back then, my dad's drinking was little more than a predictable backdrop. Just wine and beer, around us at least. Nothing nerve-wracking. No cause for concern. Sure, he didn't come home until the early hours once or twice a week, but all dads did that, didn't they?

Mornings were our happiest times. I could trace their shape, eyes closed. My days began like this:

- get up first,
- put on school uniform,
- go downstairs to make tea and Weetabix,

- clear an alcove in the junk across our paint-stained table,
- forage for yesterday's *G2* (*The Guardian*'s mag, erudite as it got) snuck home from my dad's office.

Life unfurled in a hushed sort of way, pottering around our dusty, draughty semi on a cul-de-sac of ten. We were all friends. Even the snails, who trailed glitter on the floorboards. Even the silver birches, who painted with our mellow Welsh sun. The artists' quarter. BYOB. Bring your own brush.

Very occasionally, my routine faltered when the magazine wasn't to be seen. I rummaged, unable to enjoy my milk-sodden cereal without reading material, until—

'Have I ever let you down?' my dad asked, bolting into the kitchen.

A beat-up briefcase in one hand, a baton of inky promise in the other. He, too, had a uniform of sorts. Holey joggers and that black top with its leering, peeling hobgoblin. Barefoot, all of us. Nonsense, really, but that's the way it was. We mocked slippers. Hardiness was not optional. We didn't hydrate, either. I've never seen my mum drink water. It was all an endurance test to pass.

I pored over the crossword while my dad filled the kettle and flicked on his Roberts radio. We eased into the breeze of Taylor's rich aroma and the lapping waves of the *Today* programme. First he took up a *cwpa* cha for his long-suffering wife, our unruly mum. When it came to tea, she was uncompromising: Twining's teabag, doorstep full-fat milk, soft Welsh water, in that order. Then back downstairs for his ramshackle cafetière. And to fetch a wad of toilet roll for the pool of cat wee by the table leg. It never occurred to me that I could mop it up.

Next on his list, breakfast-in-bed delivery for Danny. Or Lord Farquaad, as we sometimes called him. Dark hair, pale skin. Scrawny until his hefty diet caught up with him in his twenties. On weekdays, our dad handed him a *pain au chocolat*, a *p.a.c.* as we called it. On weekends, bacon butties, kippers, or a full Welsh. Whatever the day, my brother sat hunched, glued to his football magazines with the chalky green eyes he received from my mum and Grandma. I had my dad's deep brown eyes, and Bee came along with a diplomatic shade of hazel.

'Where are all my things in the house?' his Lordship called out to anyone passing his room.

'Everything's in its place,' we replied, by rote.

Finally, our dad prepared marmite on bread for Bee, his Cherry Pie, by far the sweetest of us. A mass of knotty coppery curls, giggles, and kindness.

After this, I turned my chair towards him. Time, finally, to discuss our latest findings into the Ultimate Question: what's it all about?

It was an inquiry that felt most urgent to him between the hours of eleven and six, while he earned money as a lawyer with stratagems and ruses. As Ian Dury and the Blockheads hissed, what a waste. He trod water for thirty years. It must have been exhausting. On this, the evidence is overwhelming. For example, an email thread he forwarded me when I, too, was a grown-up. The first message was from his mate who worked in the block opposite:

FW: Give Us a Wave

Tue 2 Feb 2016 07:31 AM

Good Morning

Give us a wave!

My dad replied to him within three minutes:

>   Tue 2 Feb 2016 07:34 AM
>
> *Not waving but drowning.*

'Well, yes, we found your dad's choice of career puzzling,' his oldest friend, my godfather, told me later in life. Around midnight, it was. We were a few pints in at The Rose & Crown, Oxford.

'He was so creative. But there was a certain sense to it, him turning to the law,' my godfather went on. 'You see, your dad and me, we were the poorest kids at Barry Boys' Comp. I imagine he didn't want that for you lot.'

At what cost, I wondered. Our dad gave us everything he could, but what did it take from him? One weeknight, there was a thunderstorm and he ran laps of the garden, whooping. We steered clear of asking, 'How was work?'

Usefully, though, he happened to be able to conjure top-notch corporate/commercial contracts. The breweries deemed him the real deal. Yes, you read that right. A man who would die of alcoholism made a living from the beer business.

'Clever as they come, your dad,' one of the firm's equity partners told me. 'Any crack-team down from London, he could run rings around the bunch of them.'

Even Buena Vista Social Club sauntered straight to him, hiring his expertise as a notary public while in town for a concert. They pulled up, a blur of canotier hats and fat cigars, and whirled his secretary Carol around the office. He and my mum went along to that night's show.

Those brains of his were a blessing and a curse, breeding an arrogance that swelled year on year. A sense of omnipotence, an untouchability. I suppose he left humility behind in childhood.

The more senior he got, the less he bothered with a suit or a shave. His preference was to slouch off to work in stubble, cargo pants, and muddy daps. He rocked up last and left first. Took the longest lunch-breaks, too, mooching over to E. Ashton Fishmongers (est. 1800) to catch our dinner from their tilting trays of crushed ice. That slippery, silvery space at Cardiff Market's gateway was a mainstay of our meals.

He and the jovial, white-coated lads at Ashton's went way back, sharing the latest baby snaps from their wallets while my dad ordered his sprats or mackerel, my sole or salmon. A shovel of cockles to eat now, please, ta, dashed with vinegar and white pepper at the side-counter, where the smeared mirror live-streamed proceedings in reverse. If only it were archived.

He kept his white plastic bag of raw fish in the office fridge all afternoon. Answered to nobody.

'Gang of one, me,' he said to those of us who surrounded him.

As a child, I loved joining him at Ashton's on Saturdays. When our mum took us into town for clothes or shoes, we congregated at the fishmongers before a pub lunch at The Old Arcade. He pointed out the precise fish he wanted and gave a thumbs-up after each weighing. He took them as they were, whole. He didn't shirk the messy bit, no sir, littering scales and guts across our kitchen.

Meanwhile, I watched the person at the centre of it all: the woman in the glass box. She handled the till. Fishmongers slid across the brown tiles, coming to her to close every sale, passing her the money and waiting as she doled out the change. On weekends it was noisy, fast-moving, and amid it all the woman in the glass box exuded calm, composure. Nobility, even. She had her work cut out. Everyone paid cash in those days. The only time I ever saw my dad use his card was when he went to a hole-in-the-wall to get more notes to spend on us.

~

At home, in the mild swill of sunrise, when it was just him and me, my dad whirred with talk and ideas. We chatted right over the droning of the Reverend on *Thought for the Day*. Everything our family did was doused in irreverence.

'There's a new NTW play we could see, fancy it?' he suggested.

I replied, unerring, 'Defo, sounds cool to me.'

Mornings were seasoned with his many refrains, like when his pencilled checklists spilled onto two sides: 'I'm a great believer in getting things done ... just not a great practitioner.'

Ah mornings, a world raucous with dawn chorusing. My dad and I watched our old mate, the robin, conducting from his bird-table podium.

'See the beauty,' he mumbled, as the sun gushed over the rooftops and our kitchen became a canvas, the birches' artwork.

The reliability of mornings gave way, with regret, mind, to the pot luck of evenings. These weren't to be trusted. The later it got, the greater the gamble.

What was for tea? Anyone's guess. Sometimes, a microwave meal consumed in our rooms. Bland, soggy. Lukewarm. Sometimes, we ate at the caff off Wellfield Road. Our mum ran us down in her skip on wheels. She liked to drive on a tank close to empty, coasting down Penylan Hill. The speakers bellowed *Go Your Own Way*, Fleetwood Mac. At the caff, smoke-clogged til '07, I ordered jacket potato and read magazines off the rack.

Sometimes, when our dad came home in time, it was fish from Ashton's. Or the jackpot: the five of us, all together, up at The Tŷ Mawr. A pub nestled in the misty hills, where peacocks roamed and our cityscape shimmered on the horizon.

On these blissful nights at The Tŷ Mawr, my universe was nothing less and nothing more than Coca-Cola through a stripy straw and my family's burble around me. Homeward bound, our mum drove. Danny up front. Bee and I sprawled across the backseat, heads resting on our dad's knees. He smelled of fiery pink toothpaste and SA Gold hops. We giggled the whole way.

Once home, he nipped down the shed and, after a while, re-emerged to build a roaring fire. We slept soundly on these evenings in his presence. When we were small, we begged him to carry us up to bed and *cwtch* for story time.

'Up the wooden shush-a-byes, one, two, three, Daddy and his baby girls,' he sang to me and Bee.

'We're not babies anymore,' I retorted.

'Ah, you'll always be baby to me,' he said, even when we were big.

Sleep wasn't so forthcoming, quite a bit more agitated, let's say, on nights when he was out at his mystery functions. Elsewhere, with men who did business that slushed well after the M4 rush hour. We listened out, ears pricked.

Rat-a-tat. Oh, just Megi the Woo. Our witchy black cat. She used the knocker. She turned up one day, before I was born, and moved in of her own accord. She was like an older sister to me. We had five cats for most of my childhood. My mum accumulated animals: dogs, rabbits, guinea pigs, chickens, stick insects, you name it. I dabbled in rodents during primary school. A short-lived hamster, and five mice I let scurry up and down my arms. My campaign for a chipmunk was strangely fruitless.

Our door was wide open to waifs and strays. One day our mum and Danny bumped into a polecat and, naturally, brought him home. He enjoyed tucking himself under our settee and greeting us with war dances. Frizzy hops that my mum said was play. The internet said it was to confuse prey, but I didn't know what to believe.

A pot luck, the lot of it. On our dad's absent evenings, we lay still below our duvets. Listening out and hoping, if not believing, that he'd come home soon and say *nos da*, goodnight, see you in the morning. After all, there was always the morning.

chin to chest

Our dad dedicated every Sunday to the three of us. Almost dreamlike these days, the rippling memories of how our Sundays used to be. First, we swam. It was a five-minute drive to our pool at Heath Sports and Social Club, part of that hospital where Danny, Bee, and I took our first breaths. We had membership through our mum, who was a nurse there. ICU, no less.

As our neighbours set off through Nant Fawr Woods to church, into the car boot went our dad's peeling green sports bag stacked with towels, bathers, Nizoral, and scavenged goggles. Our usual trick was to nab stray eyewear from the lost and found box.

'Take what you can,' was another of his refrains, this one pinched from Captain Jack Sparrow. Why buy goggles when there are scraps up for grabs?

We nearly always had the pool to ourselves. We felt it belonged to us. Any intruders who did make the error of waddling in on a Sunday morning soon made themselves scarce.

The floats, too, were ours. Wide yellow pancakes big enough to hold us all, blue twisty tubes to bend into seats, red bricks to scoop off the floor.

If I reach as far back as I can, there I am, clinging to the shallow-end steps, while my dad beckoned, reckless in the open water. I shivered, sulky, and shook my head dolefully. There were sea monsters in the drains, and who knew what else was out there.

Despite the storm in our bathtub, Danny was at his happiest when bobbing about in water. Fearless. Of course, there's no way he remembers it. Danny had a gait in the water that wasn't front crawl or breaststroke but entirely of his own creation. His arms and legs flailed, haphazard, in a way that nonetheless propelled him where he intended to go. He had head-starts in our races. We monitored him unfailingly, like ospreys guarding their young.

For me, diving lessons were mandatory under my dad's strict instruction. His wisdom curved right back to the day he leapt off the tallest board, 16 feet high at the Empire. Up beside the sun, flying in the face of fear.

'Chin to chest, Soph, chin to chest,' he yelled every time. It unnerved me, the idea of knowingly tipping headfirst. I scrunched my eyes and flung myself into the unknown. The grotty goggles flooded my vision.

Once showered and dried with our too small, scraggly towels, Bee and I dawdled out. We had no sense of urgency.

'Speed of light, you two,' our dad laughed when we finally emerged, like we had all the time in the world. He and Danny always waited for us by the poster of the baby underwater. It was Nirvana, I realise now.

Off we went, the four of us, beetling down the tunnel to the hospital concourse for our weekly luxury of a chocolate bar each. This was a home from home when Danny's mind went haywire. I navigated the corridors with a smug air, shortcutting to the play area. Here I lorded it in the castle with loot from the bookcase, though they didn't replenish the catalogue as regularly as I'd have liked.

Admittedly, it was a little more daunting in the strobe-lit consultation rooms. It was there that grown-ups toyed with my brother's brain, bumping up the Epilim or lamotrigine. All those cables, stickered around his ghost-white face.

We didn't think of such things on Sunday mornings. Post-swim, we were exhilarated. Ravenous. We inspected WHSmith's array of confectionery, taking forever to choose while our dad browsed the papers two aisles over. I went for Bountys, mostly.

Next on our agenda, the drive to Barry for lunch at Nan's. En route, Radio 4 was co-pilot. Just in time for our favourite show, *Just a Minute* (without hesitation, repetition, or deviation). And as the *Minute Waltz* faded away, I was already deep into whatever I was reading on the backseat. The safest kind of dive. I never felt carsick. If we begged well enough, our dad detoured to St Fagans for a loaf warm from the oven.

'Right, quick as we can,' he said, locking the car. 'Ten minutes, in and out. Don't tell Nan.'

We raced up the steps of our nation's history museum, hung a left to skirt the red farmhouse from the Gower, slathered in oxblood-lime pigment and defended from witchcraft by a rowan tree.

'Say hi to your mates, Danny!' we giggled on passing the round pigsty from Pontypridd. Its stone-layered dome could be mistaken for a beehive by those not in the know.

At last, there it was: Derwen bakehouse from Aberystwyth, where farmer Evan Jenkins had built it as a communal oven of sorts. Unlike the housewives of yore, we didn't bring our own dough.

If we ventured further, we'd get to Rhyd-y-car Terrace, six miner's cottages from Merthyr Tydfil. One of these 1900s freeze-frames had once prompted my mum to mumble, 'Would've been what Grandma grew up in.'

Wires were crossed, and I spent school trips standing territorially in the doorway of what I thought was quite literally our ancestral home. Friends swung on the roped-off entrance while I pointed out our white china dogs, pigeon-cot, staircase by the fireplace, table laid for tea.

'Weren't we tidy,' I beamed with pride.

So there we were, on our greedier Sundays, at the bakehouse, plucking smudgy fistfuls of dough from inside the crust. The loaf was hollowed out by the time we got back to the car.

We zipped across the train tracks, past Ely, through Wenvoe, onto Port Road and into Barry, where he was raised in Gibbons Down.

'Hello my loves,' Nan trilled as we let ourselves in.

Danny first, then me and Bee. Our dad trailed behind, laden with his baggage from the boot. Books, papers, pens, printouts, notebooks. He was never without his contraptions.

'We been St Fags,' Danny let slip immediately.

'Don't tell me, you've been snacking.' Nan wiped her hands on her peach pinny and hugged us.

Behind her, dishes *popty-ping*ed *ping*ed *ping*ed from the microwave, whirling out piping hot. The kitchen smelled of sprouts, thawed and boiled in salt, ready to melt in our mouths. I kicked off my shoes and plodded into the living–dining room where Big Mike sat jolly at the far end of the white-clothed table, stretched from circle to oval for Sunday best. Big Mike was Nan's brother. A retired carpenter, his tufts of white hair fluttered as he guffawed at us. We were always funny to him.

'Eh, the rabble have arrived!' he cried out. 'Alri?'

Grandad shuffled out of his dappled navy-grey armchair and quivered a sparrowy hand in greeting. His eyes whispered delight at seeing us, belied by his quiet 'hello, hello' to us.

I dug my thumbnail into Nan's foaming, flowering wallpaper while everyone and everything fell into place. Each of us had an exact seat and an exact concoction of food on our plate. For instance, Grandad had mint sauce with his beef, and Danny had chips instead of veg. None of us offered Nan help, which seems odd only in hindsight. Manners weren't part of the package.

It was a place of repetition, right down to the meals. Take Grandad's daily menu:

PG Tips and a chocolate digestive,
cornflakes,
corned beef sandwiches,
meat and veg, plus a mince pie (home-baked) (all year round).

Deviation came when they went up the Tinny. 'Tŷ Newydd,' I'd unabbreviate pompously, though Welsh had been belittled into a foreign tongue in this bit of Wales. It was the pub up the road, where they and lifelong friends got tipsy on laughter and a widely shared bottle of wine.

They barely drank. Grandad was pretty much teetotal. Over on the other side of the family tree, my mum and her brother no longer touched the stuff, while Grandma's bedtime was accompanied by an ample mugful of rum. A bit like a yo-yo, perhaps, the way it loops:

Parent restrained,
child loose.
Parent loose,
child restrained.

The conversation over Sunday lunch was not what you'd call organic. Here, too, Nan did the heavy lifting. Reticence was in the men's blood. She asked about their weeks and got grunts if she was lucky.

Big Mike brought Shiraz. My dad poured three glasses for him, Nan, and Big Mike, then half a glass for me. I added a splash of water like the Romans. For as long as I could remember, I was included in the rounds. He put mini-bottles of Jacob's Creek in my stocking, as well. I never asked for them but it struck me as proper grown-up, like I was part of his club. I know I felt this way from another entry in *Sophie's Memoirs*, the week after my sixth birthday:

> *One night I stayed up until eleven o'clock eating moules and drinking wine with mum and dad.*

In Barry, things happened as if scripted. Danny finished first and departed without a word, taking his football catalogue to the settee. Bee crawled below the table to cross-tie Big Mike's shoelaces. He pretended to fall for it every time. My dad topped up the wine glasses.

Lunch eaten, the men hunched over the crossword. Grandad bought the paper first thing from the petrol station each day. He had filled in as much as he could, aided by his encyclopaedia, which lived dogeared, doggedly by his side.

My dad and Big Mike took a shot at any gaps while Grandad hovered, shifting from one foot to the other. He returned to the TV now and again, flicking between the racing on Channel 4 and Teletext for the footie scores.

I entertained myself with their *TV Choice* mag. An in-depth study, front to back. My curiosity piqued at Babs Kirby's *Your STARS*, glinting with clues about what was in store. I beelined to Leo for titbits such as *loved ones are difficult to pin down but, equally, so are you.*

Nan made teas. My dad's older brother Steve arrived on cue. He never took off his daps, instead chuckling at our kicked-off shoes under the stairs. 'What's this, eh, the local mosque?'

His kids grew out of Sundays earlier than us, but back in the day my cousin James taught me how to scout for leftover coppers in the bowels of slot machines down the Island. James had a real talent for it. Steve's penny-pinching was the butt of my dad's jokes. I thought Steve's cheeriness was priceless.

After the teas, which my dad left undrunk, we piled into the car to knock about a few tennis balls at Romilly Park or head to our favourite beach: Jackson's Spade (Bay). All seasons, all weathers. If the beach was not too chilly, we'd have another dip, saltwater this time. A kick-about. A search for buried treasure: fossils, driftwood, chipped pottery.

Mostly it was mild and overcast, from memory. Danny always barrelled down the steep path, past Barry Yacht Club, hurtling onto the sandy slope. The red-faced cliffs were crumbling. Nothing serious, just the occasional rock tumbling near beachgoers. Danny galloped into the water. Our dad followed, cheering.

'Best meds for your eczema, hey Danny boy,' he called, then up to me, 'Oi, you a man or a mouse?'

I tiptoed in, wincing, maybe up to my knees, waist at most, then scuttled back to the sand after a minute. All we had for getting dry were our too small, still damp towels. My teeth were percussion to the gulls' crawing chorus. I felt deference to them, birds. They outlived the dinosaurs, after all. They came first and sure did let us know this. If they wanted a chip, they got it. And here in Wales, don't forget, we had the *adar Rhiannon*, Rhi's birds, whose song could lull the living to sleep and wake up the dead.

Meanwhile, Bee looked for crabs in the rockpools. Our dad sometimes accompanied her, scouring for treasure to add to his haul. 'Art,' he called it. A heap of wreckage, squirming and swelling in our hall. Deep beneath the surface was an ancient gnarl of wood he once pinched from a skip, hammering in a layer of netting to hang his collectibles. These included a sheep skull, a broken anchor, and a Fisherman's Friend tin.

'The time has come, the Walrus said.' Another of his refrains. Hometime, this one meant.

On leaving, my dad shoved his beachy feet straight into worn-out daps. He ripped into Steve, who busily rinsed his heels and slipped on socks still clean from the wash.

We retraced our tyre marks on the return journey, sneaking back via the Heath. On nearing A&E, we played our Ambulance Game, chanting guesses of how many would be parked up. Paramedics didn't count.

'Three, three, three!' A fairly safe bet.

'Four, four, four!' More daring.

'Five, five, five!' Wildcard.

We cheered the name of whoever won, or if no one, 'Nobody, nobody!'

Pretty grim, I suppose, as family traditions go. Fair play though, it was one of our games where Danny had as good a chance as any of us. Our dad favoured activities like that. It's only now I see something else in it: a strategy, perhaps, to drown out the past as we passed. The flashbacks of Danny's body being rushed in, unblinking and fizzing with sparks.

We turned into our coldy-sack (as I once spelled cul-de-sac, to Grandma's downright horror). My mum was out the front, nursing another milk-in-first *cwpa* cha. Her red-hennaed fringe and plaits flared in the setting sun. She waved the hose vaguely around her pots while chatting over the hedge with Karim from next-door. He greeted us with his signature wide smile.

'Got any chips for us, Karim?' Danny called.

'Don't panic, Mr Mainwaring,' my mum said to him. 'You'll be having tea soon.'

Karim winked. He often dropped over a free cone after finishing his shifts at Penylan Fish Bar.

And like clockwork, there he was, Chris P sauntering out from his porch. 'Yo, coming out?'

'Out' was the street. We were out every night, playing touch rugby or mob or footie or whatever else we came up with. Five families. In hindsight, we couldn't have been less alike, but we spent our entire childhood together. I filled weeks scripting shows for us to perform for the neighbourhood, badgering people into 8 am weekend rehearsals.

Once, when we were older, we ate a meal out. *Out* out. We gathered, a ragtag bunch, at a chain restaurant in town. The server's eyes swept the table, some of us in dresses, some in tracksuits, some in jeans and polos, some in blouses and skirts. Giggling, teasing each other. She couldn't figure us out.

'Colleagues?' she asked.

Not everyone heard. Chris P was closest, replying, 'Nah, we know each other from the street, like.'

The server blinked in surprise.

'Oh, right,' she swallowed, then faltered, tapping her pen against her notepad.

I waved my hand, laughing. 'He means neighbours, we were neighbours.'

Confusion slipped from her shoulders, and she laughed too. 'Wow, yeah I *was* thinking—'

Would I still laugh now, given everything? Honestly, probably yes.

On lighter, summery Sunday evenings, my dad headed off to play golf with his mates. They went for a pint afterwards. Or two, three, four. And with that, out he swam. Further, faster, until there he was in the distance. Beckoning, reckless, from the open water. Until the morning.

I once asked Nan, out of curiosity, what her childhood Sundays were like. She wrote back promptly:

I was the third child, in 1938, just a year before war broke out in 1939.

My earliest years were during the time when bombshells were being dropped on the docks and we had to leave the house in the night to stay in the air raid shelter in the garden. I can remember peering out to see the searchlight's beams across the night sky. Windows had to be covered in blackout cloth to stop any light showing in the houses.

We were a Catholic family, and every Sunday we made our way to church together. My mother, by some miracle, as I think now, always managed to produce a Sunday dinner for five children and Mam and Dad.

We all sat down to eat together and although money must have been in very short supply, none of us remember going hungry. Everything was rationed so you had to be very careful in your choice of what was cooked. Of course we accepted everything we had, not realising how much of a struggle it must have been.

we watched the sun go down

'It's eight o'clock all over the dock, the ships are going to sea,' my dad ruckussed through the hall, plodding in, out, in, out to load the car for our regular drive to France.

Winter swept through the open door, goosepimpling my skinny arms. I zipped up my puffer. *Thought for the Day* had been and gone. Something about the coming new year and fresh starts, no doubt. I wasn't paying attention. I nibbled cheese left over from Keith's annual Boxing Day buffet. Keith was Grandma's (boy)friend.

Every holiday took place at our French house, bought by Grandad in the 80s and inherited by our mum. Born and bred in the Rhondda, Grandad was a scaffolder until Grandma made him join the police force. He worked his way up to Chief Superintendent. One time I fancied a chat with him, so casually rang 999 on our landline. It didn't go as planned.

As I got older, I begged to go farther afield but my mum was scared of flying. I didn't get on a plane until adolescence. That flight was an impulsive gift from Grandma, who let herself in early on our birthdays. We were usually still in bed. My dad sullenly made her coffee. On one birthday – was it my 11th or 12th, I don't remember – Grandma left before the rest of us emerged. Oh god, what had he said now? They rarely got on. She returned a while later, wielding a Costa del Sol brochure. She had been down the travel agents at Rhydypenau Crossroads.

'You're holding them back.' Grandma shook her head at her howling daughter.

That was to come. For now, we set off to France at 10ish. Well behind our dad's schedule, with at least one U-turn for— who knows what. The M4 was kind to us, then there was the dreaded M25 to contend with. I read books and listened to my MP3, drowning out my mum effing and blinding up front. At least there was Clacket Lane to look forward to, number-one in our service station rankings. We were loyal like that.

We reached the Port of Dover mid-afternoon and waited on the tarmac for our ferry. Lorries chugged up the ramp as the radio played and our car battery ran flat. At last it was our turn to be gulped up into the ferry's noisy belly. We scaled one of the intestinal staircases, taking no note of which, then scampered through the greasy canteen, which left oil slicks on the skin.

Straight out onto the deck we went. The wind tore sideways and we struggled to shut the door. Our dad shepherded us to the cold railings, where we bade farewell, for now, to the chalky cliffs. I leaned over, peering below. 'Dad, what would you do if I fell?'

'Silly question,' he said, peregrine-quick. 'I'd dive right in after you of course.'

As we neared Calais, we were told to please return to our vehicles, *merci*. Other parents gathered their kids and dutifully drifted carwards. I looked on, wistful, imagining what it would be like to disembark with dignity.

Our parents, no. They ignored every announcement, holding out until the last minute. Why? So we could scoop up armfuls of littered newspapers. Take what you can. They even eyed up papers while passengers were still reading them. I felt proud to land a good one. Eventually we sprinted down the wrong staircase, looking for our dad's Saab, which was, as ever, blocking the exit. Our parents were shameless. We were mortified. This is how journeys went.

Fifty minutes later, we eased open our Tardis-blue door. We swept aside the mound of publicity that had ignored our *Pas de Publicité S.V.P.* sign. Death notices, too, which my dad read aloud with dramatised sorrow.

'*Mais non*, poor Monsieur Dumont is no more. Oh, I'll really miss that guy. Never met him, mind.'

I sat on the brown-tiled doorstep, our only outdoor space, to read *Ratus écrit un livre*. My dad hummed to the muffled notes of his Berlioz record. Our neighbours kissed our cheeks as they passed on their way home, the other end of our terraced row. They had at least twice as many kids and a fraction of the means. We gave them our old clothes and they thanked us with beef bourguignon, which Danny point-blank refused to eat.

And there was our neighbour opposite, lolling on his thin, paint-peeling balcony. *Bien sûr*, of course, always there. Around my dad's age. No job that we knew of.

One time while our dad was busy painting the shutters, our lolling neighbour decided to blast 'You're Beautiful' on loop. Berlioz stood no chance. 'My life is brilliant. My life is brilliant … She could see from my face that I was fucking hiiiigh.'

Our mum sighed. 'I don't know about Blunt, but that guy is definitely fucking high.'

There came a point when our dad descended his ladder. He laid the squelching, bubbling paintbrush on the tin lid.

'*Scusez-moi,*' he called. '*Peu de calme? Pas de musique?*'

Our neighbour cranked up the volume. They exchanged less polite words and, to our shock, the man left his balcony.

Our dad raised his fist in victory. 'Showed him, didn't I.'

A minute later, a figure hobbled out semi-menacingly by the flat's entrance lockers. Danny and I ran to fill a bucket with water. Our battle plan. By the time we wobbled out, most of our weaponry spilt, our dad had beaten us to it. He had tipped his ladder into a spear, of sorts, brandishing it to force the man back indoors. No hard feelings, as it happened, and, by morning, all forgotten.

New Year's Eve was always a different sort of warfare. This year our dad was slumped, wine-sunk, in the rattan chair. The rest of them were in bed by nine, wearied sooner than usual. I studied, for a moment, the blue-grey palette of his sea-swept face. I couldn't imagine the storms that must have raged behind his flickering eyelids. He clung to his tipped glass, an empty bottle at his feet. I imagined them shattering, shards splintering our throats.

He forever left us on this night, New Year's Eve. The Stellas at lunch could have passed, as could the Muscadet with dinner. Less so the next bottle in front of the TV. At ten to midnight, I scrunched into the windowsill and wrote a list in biro of my goals for the year. A coping mechanism, I suppose.

The next day smelled of croissants from Grémont, our favourite *boulanger*. Laziest baker ever, closed half the time, but one of a kind.

It smelled of my dad's aftershave in the car en route to Le Crotoy, our favourite beach. The raw sea breeze built characters and appetites.

It smelled of butter-drenched fish frying at Les Canotiers, our favourite restaurant. We wolfed down the basket of *pain*. A waiter presented a tiered array of shellfish to a nearby table.

'Woah, check that out,' we prompted our dad. We always remembered our lines in the act of forgetting. Well-rehearsed, we were.

'One of these days,' he recited, 'you'll see, it'll be the shellfish extravaganza for me.'

And with that, he ordered his *moules-frites* and Muscadet. *Plus ça change*, eh.

Afterwards, we leaned into the estuary's brisk saline embrace. Hands entwined, our mum and dad teased the shoreline, never taking their eyes off Danny's spectral body lumbering in the shallows. The brawny current had no pity for the likes of him. Bee amused herself finding beautiful shells to present to our parents, if they got a moment. My dad hurled a pebble above the water and hit it with another stone mid-air. We cheered.

∼

A few New Year's Eves later, we drove from the French house to Paris for a treat. We carried our things from the boot and checked into an unassuming hotel. How exciting, we thought. How nerve-wracking, we realised. Within minutes, our dad was on a one-man mission to see off a bottle of sparkling wine.

'Guys, it's New Year's Eve!' he cried. 'Come on, let's live a little!'

I sat on the edge of the bed, watching him and picking my lips. Suddenly, my mind felt like it was imploding under the weight of dread. I was sick of all the unpredictability, the inability to keep hold of an evening. I put a pillow over my head and refused to move.

They left me and went to celebrate at the Arc de Triomphe. I stayed very still, my belly tight and jittering as fireworks erupted around me. I was so tired. Still a child. It was the first time I had set myself apart, refusing to play along. Standing up to him did not feel liberating. I was sad, frightened, exhausted, and alone in a city I didn't know. I had to snap out of it. The only one I was punishing was me. I sat up and read my book.

When they came back to the hotel, Bee climbed into my bed. We had a twin room next door to the family room that Danny was sharing with our parents. Bee just wanted us all to have a nice time, to be a nice family. I couldn't ruin this for her. The two of us watched *Love Actually* and copied Hugh Grant's dance moves to 'Jump (For My Love)'. In the morning we took pictures by our window, framing the grey lines of Parisian buildings. I posted these on Facebook and got a bunch of likes.

~

I've logged this trip in my memory as the first instance of a distancing between us. Me / them. At some point around then, I asked my mum if my dad was an alcoholic. He was just 'alcohol dependent', she said. I began questioning it all in my head. Mid-teens, I was no longer naive enough to think it normal that she got us to fetch wine for Grandma's aperitifs from under clothes in her wardrobe.

It didn't stop me drinking, though. I started to throw my own parties. Booming music, cheap wine slopping onto the floor. Katy Perry yelling about teenage dreams, hearts racing, skin-tight jeans. Kesha hollering not to stop, make it pop. My mum took Danny elsewhere, leaving my dad 'in charge'. He bunkered down in their bedroom with his papers and Radio 4. I can remember only one time he made an appearance. We must have dialled up the volume seriously OTT. He poked his head through the kitchen door.

'Uh, Soph—'

My friend Kate waltzed over and gave him a wink. A few of them had a thing for him. He span on his heel and fled. We never heard a peep again.

In many ways, our parents didn't really parent us. They were more on our level. Discipline wasn't their thing, even if they tried to put in a shift. Like that time when my brother spat in the sink and our dad tried to scold him. So out of practice, he mangled his words.

'Pigs shpit in the shink,' he said. We burst out laughing.

I thought of my parents as heroes throughout childhood. I learned this in AS level Welsh. The seven of us were sat in a circle in Room 9. Odd block, first floor, door on the right. Mrs Evans' domain. We were discussing the legends of Welsh culture.

'*Nawr 'te, pwy ydy dy arwr di?*,' Mrs Evans asked us. ('Now then, who are your heroes?')

She turned to me first.

'*Hm, wel,*' I fumbled, '*Uh, fy rhieni, a ddweud y gwir.*' ('My parents, to tell the truth.')

I had no idea where it came from. Somehow I heroised them despite becoming more aware of their flaws?

The same term, in another classroom, our English teacher told us we'd do best if we described a familiar situation for our AS level exam's creative writing section. She said writing from life would be more powerful than anything we might come up with ourselves.

I wrote about a dad disrupting a family's sleep in the early hours, stumbling on the steps, clattering keys, smashing pots. I described the man laugh-wheezing as his child unlocked the door for him. How the toxic fumes lingered as he staggered upstairs. How the daughter went back to bed wondering why it had to go on like this.

It didn't test me in the slightest, that exam. I barely had to think, it was so familiar. The words poured out onto the lined booklets. My teacher was right. It scored 100 per cent.

it's a different world now

School was straightforward for me, far simpler than the spiralling complexities of home. My bedroom desk was a place of safety there. I curled up with a mug of tea, looking over facts and stats already committed to memory. Predictable, stable, reassuring. I loved languages especially. I seeded words and structures in my mind, ready to bloom and grow. It gave me a pleasing feeling of control. I read widely.

Grandma and my dad had always harboured hopes that I'd 'go far'. It was one of two things that these fiery in-laws had in common. The other was their liking for wine. Even on this, though, they diverged: red for him, white for her.

'Anything but Chardonnay,' our dad groaned as his mother-in-law handed him a glass of Chardonnay.

Their hopes were tracking well. My school sent a letter home saying I was 'gifted and talented' and had 'special needs'. This framing upset my dad.

'What are they playing at, saying you have special needs?' he tossed the letter onto the kitchen table. 'I've already got one kid with special needs.'

~

One weekend, my dad laid out a suggestion. It was a Saturday afternoon. He took us kids up Caerphilly Mountain for a blustery walk. We stood on the trig point, mimicking Jesus, arms outstretched. Afterwards we went to The Black Cock, a favourite pub of ours, tucked in among the trees.

We sat in the corner of the bar area. Our dad got drinks, the usual: his ale, Danny's lemonade, full-fat cokes for me and Bee. He put in our food order, the usual. And then, something unusual. He hooked a wedge of folded A4 printouts from his back pocket and flattened them with his forearm.

'Get a load of this,' he said.

'*Classics*,' I read aloud.

'You'd have it all. Literature, history, languages, philosophy. Pretty magic, huh.'

Classics didn't mean studying the English literary canon, or even classical music. This would prove to be a major source of confusion for my teachers. Nope, what it meant was studying the Greeks, the Romans, and what they ever did for us.

'A client of mine told me he had studied it, this Classics,' my dad said, wiping Brains beer from his face. 'Didn't sound like too raw a deal to me.'

I squinted at the text, trying to decipher the strange words. *Literae Humaniores*. He had printed these pages from the website of a *faculty*. It was all a different language.

He went up for a second pint. Not that I minded at that point. No, I was angled forward in my seat, keen to show compliance. I read the paragraphs line by line over my jacket potato, cheese, and beans. He pointed to parts he had highlighted, gulping his steak and ale pie. It was exciting.

This decided it.

~

At fifteen, I did an overnight stay in Oxford for an open day. Danny and our dad came with me. We posed for photos by the Bridge of Sighs and Christ Church College, all blue skies and smiles. We looked so similar, the three of us, with our thick dark manes and narrow eyes. It was sweltering, T-shirt and shorts weather. I could see myself here, this city with its restless, obsessive energy. People here knew what was what, I assumed. I yearned to be one of them.

That evening, the three of us sat on the patio of a riverside pub. Danny and I ate chips and crunched ice in our fizzy drinks.

'You know, they call the Thames the "Isis" here,' our dad said after a glug of local ale. I nodded, filing this as a thing I must know. Hat-clad people passed in boats. We didn't know anyone who wore hats. Once I thought to try out a pink beret and asked my dad to take a photo. He took my camera then paused. 'You keeping that thing on for the picture?' I didn't attempt it again.

Sunset came late that day. We walked through University Parks as the light faded. Our dad wandered hazily, happily, gazing at the sky. I was scouring for landmarks. We were lost. I exited through a gate and hailed a cab, the first I had ever taken. The driver knew the way to our building.

Back in the room, I sat on the bed, sun-sleepy and relieved, then realised I had left my phone on the backseat. Anxiety had been distracting. I rang the taxi company on my dad's mobile and recited the number-plate. I don't know if I deliberately memorised it, but things I looked at often stayed photographed in my head. The man dropped it back a few minutes later. It was a strange end to a strange day.

~

That autumn I went to Oxford again with a friend for a weekend. Blue skies, smiles, all over again. Was it always like this here, I wondered. We ate crêpes and snuck into a *bop*, that is, a fancy-dress party in a college's beer cellar. Some students were dressed as Dalmatians. Our ordinary outfits stuck out, but we had fun.

The two of us went back for an official open day the next summer, the age when we were supposed to do such things. My friend wanted to visit Merton College. It didn't appeal to me, so I carried on ambling along the road until I was stopped by a guy with ruffly hair in a big jumper. He was behind a stand outside tall wooden doors.

'Know anything about Corpus Christi?'

'Nope,' I smiled.

'We host the tortoise fair each year.'

I laughed, unsure whether he was joking. He wasn't.

'What subject are you after?' he asked.

'Classics.'

'Oh, that's what we're known for,' he replied. 'We're the best.'

You can't find out that sort of thing on Google, I guess. He took me on a private tour up a winding staircase into the library. I paused at the front desk, where a stained glass window overlooked a chapel. That was part of the college, too, I learned. I met the gardens, wild and paradisal. The gardener's glasshouse spilled over with flotsam and jetsam and a mannequin sat tall with a bow and arrow. There was something slightly chaotic about life here. I realised I felt completely at home.

'I love it,' I said. 'I'll apply.'

~

That September, I prepared my application to Corpus Christi College, Oxford. I embraced the UCAS discount for submitting to just one place.

'If they don't want me, I'll go see the world instead!' I told my parents, precociously.

If it was arrogance, it was very nervous arrogance. I wished with every fibre of my being that it would happen even though it was a world I couldn't comprehend. Getting from Cardiff High to that enigmatic Classics faculty took years of effort but I didn't begrudge a second of it. I guess Oxford was, for me, the opposite of *hirmynd*, long going. It felt like *hirdod*, long coming.

I emailed drafts and redrafts of my personal statement to my dad, who helped me to bring it alive. Next I was asked to take the language aptitude test. I sat it in our school hall, trying to make sense of a language that the tutors had made up to challenge us. I found it fun, then terrifying. I thought the feeling of being challenged meant I had failed. I ran through Nant Fawr Woods to our empty house and cried over a bowl of pasta before returning for my next lesson.

I received an invitation to interviews and was shocked. They must have decided to give me one more chance, I assumed. I also had to post off hand-written essays, one for English and one for History. It was all they had to go by. Cardiff High didn't do Classics.

I took the train to Oxford via Didcot Parkway, then walked across the city to Corpus Christi College. A pelican tore at its feathers in the courtyard, or the *quad* as they called it. I was greeted in the Porters' Lodge by men with snowy hair and bellowing voices. One was smoking a pipe. A girl with a plummy voice introduced herself. Another Classics applicant. That was about all we had in common. She asked which A levels I was doing, then looked confused by my reply. Hers included Latin and Ancient Greek.

I was allotted an eerily beautiful bedroom. Outside the window, a clock chimed every fifteen minutes. I paced back and forth, back and forth, flicking through my tome of notes on the million things I thought might come up. I gripped tight the heavy blue folder I had nicked from my dad's office. After a while, I called Lisa and failed to hide my fear.

There were three interviews scheduled for me. One on literature, one on language, and one on both history and philosophy. I climbed what felt like 100 stairs to head into the first of these. Three tutors sat in armchairs, sipping tea. The room was warm, cosy even. I tried to seem bright and charming in my White Stuff dress and tall brown boots. I had bought these especially.

The professors focused their questions on *King Lear*, the play we had been reading for my English Literature A level. It was going okay, safe territory, until one went off-script.

'I read something about the significance of salt in the play. Could you tell us a bit about that?'

'Uh, salt? Umm ... I don't know if we've got to that part,' I mumbled, mortified.

Again, I thought it was all over. I remember nothing other than that exchange. I got into bed and ate a Bounty. More tears. Back then I never cried about anything except Oxford.

The next one went fine, blissfully. Languages were where I excelled. The third was the most memorable. I suppose I was less delirious by then.

'Is it possible to lie to yourself?' Ursula, the philosophy tutor, asked me.

My response was probably mediocre but at least didn't leave me knowingly failing. Then it was the ancient history tutor's turn. He wondered aloud how my upbringing in Wales might lend itself to my studies.

'Well, the word for "bridge" is the same in Welsh and Latin,' I ventured. 'And I love visiting Caerleon, the Roman fortress and baths.'

He lit up, telling me he used to go for runs near there when he lived locally. I left the interview and packed to go home. I boarded a train, consoling myself that I had done what I could. I jangled with question marks even so: was this goodbye or would this place soon be my new home?

~

One snow-swept morning just before Christmas, our weary postman slung a letter into our hallway. I held it, unopened, in my right hand over the three miles I trudged in my wellies to St Edeyrn's churchyard. I wanted to read it somewhere peaceful and quiet. Just me and the presence of my kind, gentle grandad, who had been buried there in 1999.

The letter brought me what I had dreamed of. Somehow I cried a third time, now with joy. We went to The Tŷ Mawr for lunch, then I went clubbing with Lisa. We danced until the early hours, shrieking across the pounding music and downing shots like the giddy seventeen year olds we were.

I came home to a poster Blu-Tacked to my bedroom door, handmade by Bee and our dad.

It's a different world now, he had written in thick marker pen.

I read it through tequila tears. It was among the most surreal dawns of my life. I would be the first to study at a real-life uni. My dad had gone to a polytechnic, my mum to nursing college. Did it sharpen that ache of isolation, me / them, or is that a figment of hindsight?

That weekend the five of us went to Lisa's for food, along with my friend Pip's family too. We sat chatting in the living room. My mum was teasing my dad about how late he had stayed out the night before. He bristled, crossing his arms, and got defensive.

'I don't see you having a go at Sophie,' he snapped. 'She was out til gone two the other night.'

I pulled a face at him, 'Mate I'm seventeen, you're like forty-something. Besides, we were celebrating.'

The conversation moved on, but it stuck in my head. I was really beginning to think our situation wasn't normal.

Whatever. Come next autumn I'd be out of here. Bee barely hid her despair, only eleven and soon to be alone in our maddeningly topsy-turvy house. Hilarious one minute, tense the next. I tried to muffle my guilt about how I'd be abandoning Bee, instead going out clubbing on weeknights and spending weekends with my then-boyfriend. I became inattentive, already elsewhere.

My Welsh teacher gave me a card when school ended. Among the things she wrote was this:

Ti wedi croesi'r bont. (You've crossed the bridge.)

She meant the shift from learner to fluent. I interpret it differently now.

As a kid, I never told anyone about my dad's drinking. We rarely mentioned it even among ourselves, certainly never in front of him. In a moment of abandon around my 18th birthday, I made a vague comment about it to my boyfriend at the time.

He frowned, 'Surely a person is only an alcoholic when their drinking is a problem.'

Talking about problems wasn't something I did, not with him, not with anyone.

'Mhm, yeah I guess,' I replied, and left it at that.

What did a problem look like? In any case, I couldn't say how often my dad drove over the limit, how regularly he reeked of alcohol when I popped into his office to print revision notes, how increasingly he drank until he disappeared.

I couldn't say anything, because saying it out loud might get him into trouble. Because once our secret was out, it was out of our control. Because if I said something, he could lose his job or get arrested. Because if I did tell anyone, he'd hate me for betraying him. Because, at the heart of it, I loved him.

And, anyway, he did so much for us. He'd give us anything, anything except that thing we wanted most: for him not to drink.

a shock to the system

It was only after I had left home that I truly understood how serious a problem we had. Up close it was hard to detect the severity, the abnormality of it all. From a distance, my mum's sob stories down the phone began to sound extremely imperfect as I walked below those too perfect spires of Oxford.

The trouble was, he was still the person I reached out to when I was happy, when I was sad, when I was anything, really. We exchanged emails continuously. Mine are full of eagerness, his of encouragement. *Bien joué*, he wrote. *Well played*.

We sent each other articles, lyrics, quotes, photos, jokes. We signed off with weird names. Sophster. The Fath. Or in French, Latin, Welsh, even our own nonsense lexicon.

He went to France often, usually dropping by Oxford, often now taking Danny. They were thick as thieves, apart from when their fists were flying. They seemed to get on best when it was just the two of them, even if it did mean our dad was responsible for Danny's twice-daily medicines. I realise he probably missed me, but he kept himself busy, upbeat mostly. I still have a card that they posted to me from there. There's an owl on the front, and inside is this:

Sophie
We are sitting in the kitchen in the French house watching the birds whilst tucking into M. Gremont's croissants and p.a.c.s. It was sunny yesterday and we went fishing in Berk Nautique. There was no wind but big waves. We watched the sun go down. It was high tide and the sky was red. We saw the beauty and stayed there until it was pitch dark. We are going to Le Croytoy today. I am definitely going to have the shellfish extravaganza; 100% sure this time. First we will do a bit in the garden and go and see my old friend Paul Whitehouse at the dump. Not so sunny today. Matthew ch. 16 wrong again. Danny's sunny disposition will have to suffice. Loads of love, Dad
Sophie is making Classics in Oxford and here I am in France with the nasty old dad who wants me to pick leaves up
Love from
Dan

~

Settling into Oxford meant a lot to learn. I was an imposter in Classics, but the degree was a piece of cake compared to everything else I had to get to grips with.

Cutlery. Clothes. Conversation. What was *supper*? Autumn term was *Michaelmas*, spring term was *Hilary*, summer term was *Trinity*. Why did people keep asking what school I went to, as if they'd know Cardiff High? They had different reference points. Posh to us was Monsoon and Laura Ashley. I hadn't even heard of the stuff that people spoke of here.

Notes to self: drop the 'y' in 'heard'; look up the meaning of *left-wing* and *right-wing*. (I pictured a grand mahogany staircase with a T-junction of steps into corridors veering left and right. Not quite.) Two friends cracked up at what I thought was an astute remark of mine.

'*The Guardian* doesn't seem to like David Cameron,' I commented.

They looked at each other, then burst into peals of laughter. 'Wow, Soph, newsflash.'

My second-hand copies of *G2* hadn't enlightened me as much as I had thought. The only politics I knew was our home's power dynamics, silent debates, and tiptoe diplomacy.

My life then was one of extremes and excess in all directions. I finished essays minutes pre-deadline then celebrated with messy nights out, pre-drinks at mine. I drank heavily, but then so did everyone I hung out with. Sometimes my sadness leaked out in the early hours, crying myself to sleep.

'You can't keep burning the candle at both ends,' Grandma tutted every eight weeks when I came home.

Sometime towards the end of my first year, drunk in the middle of the night, I felt another impulse to tell someone about his drinking.

'I think my dad might be an alcoholic,' I whispered.

'Mine, too,' the boy said, nonchalant.

Surprise jolted me. 'Does he know he has a problem, your dad?'

'Yeah, he's been to rehab,' he murmured. 'He's working on it.'

I felt a new emotion: envy. To have a dad who went to rehab, to have a dad who's working on it. What I'd have given to have a dad who just acknowledged it.

The next day, I turned up unsteady, still tipsy, to my 9 am one-to-one tutorial. I could see the professor's disappointment in her eyes. I was not fulfilling my potential.

Another morning, not long afterwards, I woke up with bleeding knees and no clue how I got home. I texted my college husband. We had all been given to parents in Freshers' week, then told to find partners to raise the next arrivals.

Come to mine, my college husband replied.

I winced as he wiped the grit off my legs. Red-eyed himself, he told me a friend had carried me home from the club. I had collapsed in the gutter after buying multiple rounds of Jägerbombs for everyone.

I left him to tend to his hangover and scurried off with my laptop to a coffee shop. I never had headaches or nausea, just mind-blanks and mild embarrassment. My dad never had hangovers either. The only physical mementos I had from hedonistic nights out were swollen eyes from crying about his drinking. I didn't see the absurdity at the time, how closely I resembled him, quasi-invincible and blinkered.

My antics went on until *Hilary* term of my second year, when I quit drinking altogether. I had to prepare for the world's second-hardest exams: *Mods* (Honour Moderations). Or were they the world's most gruelling, since the Chinese civil service entrance exams got scrapped?

Mods consisted of twelve three-hour exams over six days. They didn't count towards our degree, just a hoop to jump through, but I thought if I could get a First then people might believe that I belonged here, that I wasn't an error.

As with everything, I kept my dad in the loop by the day. *Strength and honour*, he wrote to me. I live-streamed any delight, lit up with exclamation marks.

Re: EEEEEEEK

Thu 24 Jan 2013 9:36 AM

DAD DAD DAD DAD I just had a meeting with our President and Senior Tutors (happens every term) and Stephen (that tutor of mine who was at the poetry reading) said that I should get a First! He said I deserve a First! Or something like that, I can't quite remember. But he basically said that a First is on the cards!!! I just went, ohmygosh I really want one! I'm in the Bod now, extra extra motivated cause if he says that I'm capable of it then I'd be so gutted not to achieve it! Just thought I'd share the excitement hahahaha x

My dad replied within five minutes:

Thu 24 Jan 2013 9:41 AM

Utterly amazing. If you keep working like you have been, I have no doubt they are right. Just been listening to IOT. Romulus and Remus – v. Interesting. Mary Beard was on.

I was too busy, too self-involved to notice my dad was getting worse. He said it outright a few days later. I had sent him a YouTube playlist, and his response closed with a line that affects me only now I reread it:

Re: Musing-music

Mon 28 Jan 2013 2:33 PM

Yes, I recall the Prince of Egypt music being very stirring. Still can't understand how you can cope with music + work but glad you are enjoying it. I am having a nasty time fighting the forces of darkness, me.
Sum ipse patrem te

It seems from the email chain that I didn't respond to his fight, obsessed only with my own. Perhaps I thought he was talking about work. Perhaps I didn't think about it at all. A few days later, full stops and sad faces.

Re: Newyddion sbwriel

Tue 29 Jan 2013 4:27 PM

Disheartened. I only got 64.5 in my other collection: one of my essays on Greek stuff was rubbish. Doesn't help that I saw the boy next to me had a 70. This means war. I need to amp up the effort absolutely loads if I have ANY hope of achieving that First in Mods.
:(

Sad elder daughter,
Soph x

Tue 29 Jan 2013 4:29 PM

But I did find those hilarious photos in my pidge today (what do I look like?!?) which was a glimmer of brightness on an otherwise murky morning. Danke schön!

My dad's response was typically quick and spot on:

Tue 29 Jan 2013 4:52 PM

Cheer up. Don't be sad. It can't go according to plan all the time. As I sometimes say in these situations, "Ignis aurum probat, miseria fortes viros" – "fire tests gold; adversity tests strong men" [and women].
The Fath

Tue 29 Jan 2013 5:16 PM

It's alright now – my state of sadness was transient; I've moved onto listening to uplifting songs and planning my next move. (What a Feeling, Irene Cara.) Currently rereading Cicero's In Catilinam IV to regain my confidence as my tutor said Latin was my very best thing, and I've written out a list of Things to Take from the T&C Paper – the 64.5 – and hopefully I'll get lift-off beyond the ghastly 60s in the real thing. The show must go on!!!
Hope all's well. Your b-day present is on its voyage to Cymru as I type (at least it should be).
Re-inspired elder daughter,
Soph

I remember now, reading these, how much words meant to me when they came from him. He was my support network. Who was his?

That month, I was invited to a friend's birthday drinks at a cocktail bar in Jericho. I ordered a virgin Moscow mule. The party was appalled. They urged me to have one, go on, one couldn't hurt. I sipped the sickly sweet mocktail and shook my head, stubborn on the surface, conflicted inwardly. I wanted to please my friends, not to spoil the gathering. I hated letting them down.

It was easier to be elusive, encountering others only accidentally when ferrying books between my room and the library. The exception, my only socialising, was a daily run first thing with a housemate. Each afternoon I sat alone in my favourite café, Combibos, on Gloucester Green to savour a lemon and poppy seed muffin.

My Mods came and went uneventfully. My sobriety ended moments after the final exam. We sprayed each other with warm Prosecco, then descended to the beer cellar for another memoryless night.

My mum stopped dropping me off and picking me up between the short Oxford terms. She couldn't. Assured of her absence for half a day, he'd be off his face by her return. We couldn't risk it, what with Danny's temper becoming less manageable.

No big deal. I drove myself instead, pressing down my little blue Citroen's pedal along the M4. I felt mature, watching my mates head out for lunch with their parents. Me, I inhaled lattes and tuna melts at Combibos. I was always happiest when hurrying along on my own timetable. There were things to be achieved. This must be what freedom feels like, I decided.

The longer I was away, the grimmer the updates from home. My mum vowed to leave my dad more and more frequently. I believed her once, after a very bad episode, but even then she clung on.

'I love him,' she said, by way of explanation.

~

On holidays I saw first-hand how the tides were turning. I felt the paradoxical desperation each time I agreed to another trip with my dad. We still went a lot to France but sometimes beyond, too, emboldened since that Costa del Sol getaway. After my Mods, the two of us went all the way to South Africa for a road trip between Cape Town and Port Elizabeth.

I hoped our travels could be a way to broaden his horizons, like he did for me. To prove to him how much more there was to life than wine and pints. And yet, the further we went, the further any hopes of healing seemed from reality. I remember it intensely, like I'm still there with him. March, 2013. Heathrow. Even before boarding, he was sinking glass after glass in the airport lounge. He had really splashed out. We were flying business class.

'It's complimentary,' he hushed my worried stare. 'Take what you can, eh.'

He was drunk by the time we boarded. We were welcomed to our seats with trays of champagne or orange juice. I pointedly took a juice. My dad reached for the bubbles. Once we were out there, the daytimes were fun, as long as I shunted to one side the dread of dusk. One morning we impulsively decided to climb Table Mountain. We asked a shop assistant how to get to the starting point for Skeleton Gorge. We must have looked like a pair of jokers.

'This route is for serious, experienced hikers. Not amateurs,' he said bluntly, holding out a map for us.

It was an irresistible invitation. We parked and set off up Skeleton

Gorge. No food, a fast-crumpling plastic bottle of water, and a dab of suncream on our noses.

Damp from sweat and waterfalls, we clambered rope ladders and emerged through a canopy halfway into the sky. At the summit, my dad took a crumpled Welsh flag from his pocket to wave in triumph. Our red dragon roared against the diamond sky. Thank god we had remembered the essentials.

We descended at sunset, making up our route as we went along, wondering where we had left the car. Darkness was edging towards us.

That night we were seated at a restaurant, worlds away from The Tŷ Mawr. My dad ordered a bottle. When it arrived, I was caught between not wanting to encourage him, nor let him drain the whole thing, nor put a downer on his evening. It was a conundrum I grappled with each night. He poured me a glass and I saw it pleased him. The semblance of solidarity churned in my gut.

We started chatting with a couple on the table next to us. A man, loud and obnoxious, and a woman, wordless and amiable. They oozed wealth in a manner that intrigued my dad. I realised I hadn't been keeping tabs on the wine when he began repeating himself. The woman's expression turned concerned, eyes creased in sympathy. It was the most she said all evening. I felt older than all of them. I was nineteen. My dad ordered more, but I interrupted and requested the bill.

He glared, 'Ignore her, the Pinotage. A large glass.'

The couple turned away, finally too embarrassed to string out the conversation any longer.

'I need the toilet,' I said.

I stopped the waiter as I passed the bar. 'Please don't bring that wine.'

'Sorry, really, miss,' he said. His hands were tied.

Later I walked fast when we left, at last. My dad swayed ten feet behind.

'Hold your horses,' he called.

I lost it and yelled how fed up I was. I don't remember his response, probably some jokey quote, like 'Calm yourself, Iago.' Was I being a brat? Here we were, in the southern hemisphere, and I couldn't just lighten up. I ran off, frazzled, through the V&A Waterfront. He would catch up with me sooner or later, unless he got lost in the night, detouring to other bars where selfish kids wouldn't try to deny him his wine. We were sharing a twin room. My dad would never hurt me, would he, but this drunk guy? I didn't trust him.

He knocked the hotel door not long afterwards, and fell straight asleep.

Do not go gentle, a District 9 museum told us the next day, with drunken echoes, echoes of a poet we all know.

The day after that, an ostrich crossed the road at the Cape of Good Hope. I leapt out of the car to get closer.

'Woah, Soph!' my dad said as I ran up to it. 'They can be dangerous.'

It must have been an inheritance, such recklessness, or maybe there was no space to be wary of anything else. Nothing besides his drinking really frightened me at that time.

After a few more nights of this, I stopped speaking. I went completely mute. He left me to my book one afternoon in Stellenbosch, off to 'see the sights'. This was his trip of a lifetime. I felt like I was ruining it. Why the hell did I agree to come to a wine region with an alcoholic? He had always dreamt of going wine-tasting. I couldn't bear the prospect and he didn't push it. I don't know whether I regret this. He drank anyway, whether I tried to obstruct it or not, but I suppose I didn't know just how futile my efforts were back then.

I only broke my silence when I was too tired and bored to go on.

'Are you sorry?' I asked.

'Yes,' he said.

'Say it then.'

'Sorry.' A first.

I smelled it on him even then. I asked if he had been drinking. He said I was crazy.

He confirmed my suspicion later, not that I let on. I didn't have the stamina to sulk any longer. I saw how he knew his way around the bar that we went to for food, how the bartender greeted him. I said nothing. The Springboks were on TV. We watched the game with a neutral air. I sipped my coke and chewed the ice cubes.

I did feel crazy with all this guesswork and pretence. I wished I could believe things my dad said, instead of the pair of us kidding ourselves to keep a veneer of peace.

At Plettenberg Bay, we threw our things onto the sand and skeltered towards the water, heedless. It was overcast and windy. Their autumn, a coolness in the air. We were the only people on the beach. We dived into the water. By the time we thought to look back, the tide had crept in and submerged our phones, car keys, his wallet, my camera. Miraculously, they survived. Any thought of sharks didn't occur to us.

We ended the trip at a luxury safari lodge. On our last night, I connected to Wi-Fi in the lobby and saw an email with my Mods results. The yearned-for First. My immoderate approach meant I did belong in that odd, solitary world. I ran down to our villa and flung open the door.

'Dad, I did it. The First. I did it.'

I burst into tears and he hugged me, tearing up himself.

'I had no doubt you would,' he said.

The lodge was hosting a BBQ. My dad told everyone what I had achieved, then drank countless glasses of wine. I had a few, too. Anything not to spoil this moment.

Throughout our ten days together, his consumption was endless. Every night was damage control. Just before our return flight, he said he needed the toilet. I gave him a grace period, then turned to look. There he was, necking wine at the self-service bar. There was an urgency, a nervous energy, the persistence of a person anticipating being denied as he drank. I was insulted that he took me for such an idiot. Then again, it's hard trying to fool yourself and everyone else at the same time.

On the plane home, he gazed out of the window. A storm was thrashing with lightning below us. A frenzy of electricity.

'Man oh man,' he said, 'I can't wait to visit again. What a place.'

I got home exhausted. I returned to Oxford, and he emailed the following week.

Shamwari

Tue 2 Apr 2013 12:31 PM

Bit of a shock to the system to be back. I was waking up at 3.00am for a couple of mornings following our return, looking forward to seeing the rhinos etc. At least the sun is shining today.

You can probably guess, he didn't get his second visit. Not in this lifetime, anyway.

black hole

Our dad's drinking always affected us most while we were away, or maybe it was the change of scene that made those episodes so memorable. Or perhaps he drank that much daily and we just weren't there to see it. During one lunch on our summer holiday in 2013, he called me a 'fascist'. I had asked under my breath if he really needed yet another beer. I was getting more vocal, more confrontational. He looked daggers at me and said I had no idea about life.

'You don't have a clue. This is completely normal,' he retorted. '*This is nothing.*'

He ordered another beer. Then he started harrumphing when the waiter passed with a larger beer glass for another customer. On the way back to the holiday home that night, he vanished. My mum fretted in the kitchen, back and forth, *cwpa* cha after *cwpa* cha undrunk.

'What if he's fallen off the cliffs?' she agonised. 'Should one of us go looking for him?'

Danny was in bed. Bee and I should have been in bed.

Our dad came back late. Our mum ranted and he raved, twisting the blame so it looked like anyone's fault but his own. His arguments were pitiful, particularly for a lawyer.

The next night he barely spoke when he had run out of beers in the holiday home. Alcohol was by then an urgent need for him, more than a nice-to-have. We were no longer enough. I knew this now, but I wasn't sure what to do about it.

It wasn't ignorance on his part. Clearly it upset us, but we had to fall in line. He had no intention of giving up drinking. He didn't view it as a problem to be fixed. In his head, we were the bad guys. He'd get away with it if it weren't for his meddling kids.

He chose not to dwell on how it now tormented us. He wasn't the one to comfort Bee while she cried herself to sleep on his nights out. He wasn't the one to calm Danny's obsessive angst when our dad was put to bed drunk, 'No, no, don't worry, Dad's drinking won't kill him.' He wasn't the one to reason with his wife, head in hands at the sink, lamenting every bottle he downed in the shed. This isn't self-pity or self-praise. There was so much I didn't do.

~

One thing I did do, shortly after I turned twenty that summer, was an attempted intervention.

'You're the only one who could get through to him,' my mum was always telling me at the time.

'It's true. If he'd listen to anyone it'd be you,' Grandma said, sipping her Chardonnay, head tilted in a refined, withering pose. It was an angle she often held when discussing her son-in-law.

It was all down to me, I thought. I spent days writing him a letter in third person, centred around one of his disappearances on that latest holiday. I closed with these lines:

He had been my hero figure. Fun, clever, optimistic, witty, generous.

But the picture changed, and blurs further with every slurred word. Is this what his life will amount to: a haze of drunken days and nights one after the other til his kidneys fail, his liver shrivels, and his heart gives way? He could look forward to the best decades of his life. Retirement travels and games with grandchildren all frittered for more stashed flasks of spirits.

Maybe I should be more resilient at holding onto my anger when he has humiliated us or hurt us, or even just at the humdrum, blasé way that he seems drunk every hour of every day now. The trouble is that I am 'ludicrously optimistic', as an old friend once said. I always had this dream that someday he'd see the alcohol for what it really is: less a crutch, more a cane.

He used to say we had won first prize in the lottery of life. These days the drink is blinkering him to our relatively blissful lot. He acts like he hates us, while more than anything we just want the childhood version back. Tearing up that lottery ticket in a never-ending intoxicated paralysis versus regaining loved ones' trust? What's more, regaining himself? In his own words: it seems like a no-brainer.

I cringe now on rereading these harsh, sharp words. That disquieting warning about his heart, a decade in advance, the too true threat of frittering away time with grandkids.

I ended the letter with a request to meet me the next day at Coffee #1, the branch by his office. A three-hour window seemed fair. I sealed it in an envelope addressed to my dad at work, marked *CONFIDENTIAL*.

I ran downstairs and up Bettws-y-Coed Road to the post office, where I bought a single first-class stamp. Before I could stop to think, I dropped it, heart thumping, into the letterbox. His car passed me as I walked back. He slowed and I jumped in. My light-hearted chatter didn't quite drown out the churning in my gut.

It was an anxious twenty-four hours of imagining scenarios. The next day I took my place in the coffee shop, trusting the postal service implicitly. I chose a seat facing the door, then ordered a latte and opened my book. I had a reading list to get through before my Oxford term resumed, but I mainly studied the café entrance. At the halfway point, I bought a Welsh cake and tea. Two hours in, I began to consider the possibility he might not be joining me.

Totally wired by caffeine and nerves, I checked the time again on my phone. A few minutes remained. Nearly three hours had gone by and he hadn't shown up. I placed the screen face-down. The prospect of outright failure was alien to me. Then there he was, in the doorway. My heart leapt and I jumped to my feet.

'Dad! Over here.'

He hesitated, and I beckoned him to the till, 'What do you want to drink?'

He shook his head at the chalkboard, 'What even is all this stuff? Mocha – what?'

'I'll get you an Americano, go sit.'

I beamed at the bemused barista and waited at the end for our drinks, glancing over to check he was still there. I carried across our tray and nudged his coffee towards him, then began businesslike.

'Thank you for coming,' I said. 'I'm so glad you're here.'

From my tote bag, I fished for the Alcoholics Anonymous pages that I had printed at the big library in town. I laid out the papers in front of him, flattening them with my forearm. I wanted to do what he had done for me that blustery day in the pub up Caerphilly Mountain. I wanted him to find meaning in what I was showing him, to guide him towards the brighter future he deserved.

'You have to HALT,' I read aloud, 'if you're ever hungry, angry, lonely, or tired, and feel like you need a drink. Instead you could try to eat something, or calm down, or come and find us, or sleep.'

Learning all this felt more vital than my uni reading list, with higher stakes than the tests I would face there on my return. And yet I was so adrenalised that I remember just one thing he told me at that table.

'When I drink red wine, it's like a black hole,' he said. 'I can't stop.'

I nodded, excited that he was opening up to me. It was the first time in our family history that any of us were having a proper conversation about it.

The coffee shop was shutting. I hugged him. He went back to his desk, I think. My mum fetched me and took me to Grandma's, where they demanded a debrief.

'It did feel like a breakthrough,' I concluded, jubilant, on the face of it.

I didn't mention the red tint in his eyes, nor the fumes beneath his aftershave.

That night, I mulled over how many drinks he might have needed to make it to our conversation. The optimist in me hid the suspicion he was there merely to appease me. All I cared about was that he had read my scathing, hopeful letter and turned up. At least for a moment, he had chosen us.

If I did tell them he was drunk for it, would I have prevented him winning them over for the next ten years with his constant promises of change? Did protecting him mean condemning the rest of us?

~

Same as it ever was. The days went by, scenes on loop. We got through life on autopilot. He went on a golf trip with his mates that very weekend after our meeting at the coffee shop. Let's just say he wasn't sipping soft drinks.

My mum called me more than ever before. Daily tales of the latest fighting, drinking, fighting, drinking. Her emails to me became increasingly dire. For instance this, hurled into my inbox on a Friday night midway through my third year's third term:

relationships!!!

Fri 30 May 2014 9:24 PM

Knew it wouldn't last. Relationship between father and son deteriorated due to alcohol intake. Remind me who decided to have Danny and your father on a holiday.
When he's had alcohol, which has been a lot over the week, he doesn't 'do' Danny.
Thankfully we are going home tomorrow. I'm just about keeping it together.
Remember to include in your poem about the effect autism has on the relatives who have to pick up the pieces. The parent who drinks to blot out reality and the other parent who tries to pacify the remainder to make an attempt to be a sort of family.

The embarrassment of always making excuses and the totally impossible task of making peace in a world that is sometimes a 'living hell'. Strong words but ones which are meant in a desperate plea to write things down to maintain some sense of coping. Perhaps things really do need to change.

In our favourite game show, that last line would have failed on every count: hesitation, repetition, deviation, over and over again.

[   ]

The summer before my final year, my mum suggested I go to stay with one of my closest friends in California. I was ecstatic. I had been sad that he was leaving Oxford.

Then she suggested my dad and Bee join me. How bad could it be? I chose to forget past experience and ignore probability. We booked a hotel recommended by my friend's family, a ten-minute drive from their house. I was nervous-excited. My sister barely remembers anything from the trip. Her mind wiped it, because yes it was that bad.

I turned twenty-one while we were out there. There were beautiful moments. There always were with our dad, the beautiful mixed with the bad. You couldn't not see it. A school of dolphins swam right up to the shore, chirruping around us on my birthday. We visited great art exhibitions. We hiked around Hollywood Hills. We had some delicious breakfasts. You really come to love breakfast as an alcoholic's daughter. In the early days, that is, when you can usually count on him being sober.

For my birthday breakfast we went to a café, Julienne's. There, on the terrace in the dappled sunshine, I was content. My dad handed me an A4 envelope. Inside was a poem he had written, which I read aloud:

TO SOPHIE MARGRETTA
ON HER 21st BIRTHDAY

You have given us nothing ... except love and joy;
You were bewildered at that glittering sun, that hard, clean sky;
Gabrielle sang "Dreams Can Come True";
You won first prize in the lottery of life (not sure if I've ever told you that);
Literally born into the biggest bunch of dysfunctional losers the world has ever seen;
A big fat rat came to greet you on your first night at home;
Your first bathroom was a derelict kitchen, like a Beirut slum it was;
Rat bones strewn all over the place (good job everyone loves them);
The embers of our fire still smouldering in the morning, Radio 4 toujours:
England batting on a dry wicket at Lords and piling up interminable, dreary runs;
A discarded copy of The Guardian – where you were later to express yourself (not too literally this time I hope);

You have given us nothing but love and joy; these things are permanent.

Every morning the old man was like a streak of lightning flying across the sky;
He was like the swiftest arrow fired from a bow;
He was like the mightiest cannonball the world has ever seen;
... snorting, neighing, and limping down the stairs to make his coffee and her tea, the ravages of four and a half thousand squash matches and general decrepitude taking their toll on his old hooves;
Off at the very crack of dawn (or 11.00am at the latest) to clarify a few concepts and make a few distinctions and wonder what it's all about.

*The Valley Commando – rough as four and a half thousand bears
– your mother, not really a 'normal' Cyncoed Mum – somewhat
unconventional you might say, wonderfully irreverent, rude, wise,
and kind (mostly to animals);
Full of love and angst but the greatest mum and the finest woman
who ever lived, whatever she tells you.*

*'Where is all my stuff in the house?' A query from Lord Farquaad;
The greatest hero who ever lived – hilarious, infuriating, and
innocent but only odd on the odd occasion.*

*Guess who's next? Go on, guess. Yes it's Bee, talks too fast to be
intelligible (though I think I caught the words 'fat pig' the other
day).
She is literally the sweetest thing who ever lived, but don't steal her
food or ... guess what? She will literally stab you.*

*... and not forgetting dear Snorkie, the evil one – the most evil dog
who ever lived, with his evil, soulful eyes, would be stretched upon
the floor, dreaming of running like an evil stag and generally being
evil. Does he have any idea how much he is loved? Doubtful – he
is just a dumb, evil animal.*

So that's what it's all about then.

*But it only seems five minutes ago that we were in Pompeii ('Cave
Canem' in the Homeric House – how I wish I had heeded that
advice, battling the Beast in the Amphitheatre, the best eleven euros
and all that);
And then we would be chatting about Literae Humaniores in the
Canem Bar at the Gallum Nigrum. They chatted of very little else
there as I recall.*

So only one more year in Oxford now? Where the gargoyles climb down at night and fight with those from other colleges, or fish under the bridges, or just change their expressions overnight.

Oxford – where windows open into other worlds.

And you are twenty-one today – four and a half thousand miles away in an alien land bewildered again at that glittering sun and that hard, clean sky.

Seize the day, seize the night, and seize whatever else you can seize (and give nothing back);
Great things are not caused by those who count the cost of every thought and act;
Do everything you want to do (have I ever mentioned that I am a great believer in getting things done [and cricket]?) and go everywhere you want to go.

Thank you for everything and the fact that everything is still not ... everything.

You have given us nothing but love and joy.

I love you!
Fath.

TO ALL TO WHOM THESE PRESENTS SHALL COME:

I, [redacted] of Cardiff, a duly authorised Notary Public for England & Wales

CERTIFY that:

some of the stuff in the foregoing document is true; hopefully the most important bits; and the rest of it is a load of old rubbish.

SIGNED and SEALED at Julienne's, 2649 Mission Street, San Marino, Los Angeles, California, United States of America this 30th (or is it the 31st?) day of June (or July maybe?) 2014 (or sometime around then).

Bee and I laughed throughout. There were lots of in-jokes. My friend's family realised we were all totally mad. They invited us for dinner nonetheless. It was punchy, pencilling in an evening plan with our dad.

Predictably, he was drunk by mid-afternoon. We didn't see him drinking, but he managed it somehow. He told us the hire car keys had gone. Gone, simple as that. We looked everywhere. Under the bed, around the pool, in the restaurant. I had to get the hotel staff involved. Deep down, I knew it was a farce. I rang my friend and asked if his mum could fetch us.

Ah yes, as if by magic, our dad found them. Where? He couldn't quite say. I apologised to the staff for wasting their time. We pretended that it was fine. The evening was mellow and smelt of jasmine. We had a wonderful meal, wine, a cake with twenty-one candles. Everyone sang. We went for a gentle walk around the neighbourhood and marvelled at the neat lawns.

There were also more frightening moments on the trip. Like when we suddenly realised he was off his face in the middle of the day in San Francisco CBD. Just him, me, and Bee. Had we not been watching him carefully enough? Red-faced, squinting, he could hardly walk. We ended up storming off and leaving him alone on a random street. He didn't seem bothered. I was worried he'd be hit by a passing tram, but I guess he went for another drink or three, four, five.

Meanwhile, Bee and I took a bus to find a market I had read about online. I must have made a mistake, because we ended up on a sketchy street. Bee, aged just fourteen, clung to my arm as I tried to course-correct. We walked fast and at last found ourselves back in a touristy area, breathless and out of sorts.

The return home was a relief. At least we knew where we stood when the inevitable happened.

~

That autumn, I started my final year at Oxford. The first term, *Michaelmas*, went by quietly, and I drove back to Cardiff for Christmas. Most of the time I was in our family's house by myself, like usual. Our uni terms were short. Bee was still at school, Danny at college, our parents at work (supposedly).

One weekday my dad turned up on the doorstep, blotto. He should have been in the office, but instead he was barging against our front door's stained glass. I leaned over the banister to check I had drawn the bolt and chain, then texted my mum. She told me to ring 999. It seemed extreme to me. It was still his house, after all. I was just scared of being alone with him here like this. 'Disorderly' was the charge used by the police these days to keep him in a cell for a bit. We'd never been an orderly family, but now our disorder had twisted into something menacing. It was no longer quirky. By now it alerted authorities.

Anyway, I didn't ring. I never did, not once. Instead I locked my phone screen and sat on the top stair, peeking down and waiting until he gave up and wandered off. There's no way to describe the terror of being a traitor to the person who so lovingly, so painstakingly raised me. The risk of betrayal outweighed that of danger, I felt.

I don't remember Christmas that year. That's for the best, I imagine.

~

I went back to Oxford for *Hilary* term. One night in February I began shaking. I couldn't get the chill out of me. I tucked up close to a radiator in our college library. Friends told me I was boiling, on fire. I felt freezing. I went back to my room and began throwing up. My whole body shuddered.

The next morning my mum came to get me. I think one of my friends had called her. I could hardly walk. My head was screeching. Daylight was dizzying. The pain in my lower back was nearly unbearable. I fell on the floor when I got out of bed. I ended up in Llandough Hospital back in Wales. My dad was AWOL when I was admitted. He had been at the rugby. Phone unanswered.

They put me on the winter crisis ward with a bunch of ninety-plus year olds. I was in for five days on a drip. An acute kidney infection, caused by an untreated UTI. I hadn't been looking after myself. At night I begged for blankets, trying to shimmy away from the fans that blew cold air onto me. It was around 3 am when the nurse told me that my temperature was in the forties.

'You'll have a seizure if you're not careful,' she said.

I lay there quietly petrified. Tears slid down my face. I texted my mum to ask if she thought I was going to have a fit. Her phone was always on.

A few days later, when I was a bit better, my dad turned up unannounced with Danny. I shuffled to a room with my drip to sit with them. We had little to say to each other. My friends Lisa and Milno also visited towards the end of my stint. They bantered with the old ladies. Maisie, ninety-five or thereabouts, was convinced she was on her hols in Blackpool.

'Just off to get some rock for me grandkids,' she said every few hours, pottering off with her handbag.

'Maisie, no,' we laughed. 'Come back!'

I was let out the next weekend under strict orders to rest. Resting involved a Zoom tutorial in my PJs, a mug of tea in hand and my cat Tilly on my lap. After a few days I headed back to Oxford and posted a photo of the Radcliffe Camera on Instagram. The building looked like cake. *A flawless sky #oxford #sun #spring #HAPPY.* If Ursula, my philosophy tutor, had asked her question again, I'd have said it wasn't a case of lying to myself. Just compartmentalising, perhaps.

As a reward for my Mods performance I had been given college funds for a trip to Italy or Greece. I pictured going to Athens, alone, and said so. My mum insisted I took my dad to Rome. He had always wanted to go, she said. I had been putting off the whole thing, but now I had to use the money or lose it.

'It'll cheer him up, stop him drinking,' my mum pleaded. 'You have to take him to Rome.'

'Please don't make me do this,' I said. 'I can't do it again. Please.'

It would be a long, long time before I'd be able to say no to them, or anyone, really. I ended up having nightmares about the Rome trip for weeks leading up to it, sobbing in my sleep.

When it came to it, I couldn't do it. My dad went on my scholarship trip with Danny. I never told my college that. He emailed photos of them eating pepperoni pizza and visiting the Colosseum. I looked at their pictures from my desk, relieved it wasn't me with him. If there were any incidents between them out there, I can't remember. Or maybe I didn't ask.

~

Easter came and went, then it was my last term, *Trinity*. Our upcoming *Greats* exams would sum up our time there. All or nothing, no earlier exams counted. The immense pressure nearly broke my friends, but an unprecedented disinterest washed over me. I couldn't even pretend to care.

I milled about in cafés with notes I barely skimmed. I drank latte after latte, and sat looking around me. I walked aimlessly, photographing the city's magic. It was still sunlit, still splendid. My Instagram was all *#bluesky*, Mayfair filter. In one caption, I quoted Maya Angelou: *A free bird leaps on the back of the wind and floats downstream til the current ends and dips his wing in the orange sun rays and dares to claim the sky.* The inescapable irony of it, me portraying a life of freedom.

Instead I got lost in the news with my friend Em, also state-schooled and new to this world of spires dreaming. A General Election was called for May. The race was tight. The left-wing candidate had studied at our college. The right-wing candidate had studied at a college two cobbled streets away. I knew what these terms meant now, left-wing, right-wing.

For the first time, I cared about politics. I shared hashtagged opinions. It must have been a form of escapism from that place where my views were unwelcome. Home, where the news was worsening chaos. Violence. Vanishing acts. Police vans. My dad's drinking was landing him, us, in trouble week on week. Nowadays, it was safer if his drunken disorderliness was kept out in public. In private, things could turn nasty. Danny's anger about it was getting worse and worse. If our dad came back pissed, the household could quickly turn into a war zone.

More and more, I found myself in tears while on my own in my college room. Out of nowhere, panic spilt across the floor and rose up the walls. It almost submerged me, like I couldn't breathe beneath it. At certain moments, I no longer even believed in this glinting city, the buildings, the streets I had taken to get where I was. Life felt far-fetched, like I was imagining it. I doubted my surroundings. I doubted everything. To keep calm, I either had to be with people or keep moving. I walked quickly from library to café, café to park. I was desperate to feel light again.

I can't find any emails between me and my dad in these months.

Over in the political sphere, it was a shock defeat for our college's alumnus. The right-wing guy won with mudslinging and austerity and a referendum he didn't believe in. It was the first time I had paid attention, and it hurt.

~

I had applied to do a Master's at Cardiff Journalism School, a knee-jerk reaction to wanting to write and a mentor telling me I needed an MA to get a job at a newspaper. The two best schools were Cardiff and London, but I couldn't afford to be a student in the latter. Returning to Cardiff was a stupid idea. I knew this. My stomach lurched each time I thought about what the next year would look like, but I felt a need to be nearby, near Bee. Some friends from school would be there as well. Maybe it'd be alright? I could still back out. It wasn't a done deal yet.

One day I found I couldn't emerge from one of my suspensions of belief. I felt lost. Agitated, I got on a train from Oxford to Cardiff. It was my dad, of all people, who picked me up when I arrived in Cardiff. Why did I go there? Why not literally anywhere that was not-there? I sat numb in the passenger seat of his car, bewildered as to how I was letting myself be helped by the person I needed to escape.

The next morning, the day after I had stepped onto a train in sheer panic, my parents took me to a brick terrace. Another dead end, a few roads over from them. It was a house viewing.

'For you,' my mum said, 'when you come home.'

I stood dazed, unable to say a word. I knew I should perform gratitude, but my mind was completely blank. My mum figured I wouldn't cope if I had to live at home, but this? I didn't understand. She had always sought security in buying properties, bricks and mortar that wrought havoc with our finances. I knew I should be thankful, but this felt like a trap. Bars of indebtedness. He'd have a key. A key. A key. My heart started to beat faster. A key. A key. Little did I know, then, that the following spring my mum would send him to live with me there.

After the viewing, my mum took me to a wellness store on Albany Road. The green-aproned salesperson approached.

'Exams,' my mum said, gesturing in my direction.

'Ah, love you,' the woman cocked her head in sympathy. 'Give these a go, hun.'

She ran a jar of tablets through the till. 'Place one under your tongue at times of stress, okay love?'

I lay in Bee's bed for a day and half-watched kids' films. My sister needed me to be my old self. She brought up hot chocolate and tried to make me laugh. She was fifteen. I knew I was scaring her, but I couldn't seem to snap out of it. She wanted me to be the happy, headstrong sister she was used to. I felt so out of it.

The house purchase was spiralling without me. All I needed to do was sign, my parents said. I remember, at one point, being told to sign documents at our kitchen table. I sat still, picking my lips, looking at a biro. I refused. I was so confused. My dad threw the papers onto the floor.

'Ungrateful brat,' he said, and walked out. Probably to get smashed.

Many years later, I asked the mortgage provider for all the data they had on me from this time. A GDPR request. Somehow, as I write, I am still trapped in this enormous debt. Because, aged twenty-one, I didn't know how to run from it. The lender's call log is telling:

> *Spoke to Ms Sophie ... she said she is out of town and it is not possible for her to reach the nearest Barclays Office ... informed her that we are awaiting for signed gen signed by her ... is busy ... left a msg stating that the case is awaiting gen dec ... informed her that we won't be able to release the fund as we have not received the signed gen dec ... she will get in touch ...*

I was so young, and so dumb. Back in Oxford, it wasn't long before my mum rang with her typical reasons to be cheerful. 'He's been missing since yesterday. Dead, for all I know, or in a cell again.'

I was on the staircase of the library. My tablets weren't to hand.

'I'm sure he'll turn up,' I muttered, before hurrying back to my desk.

The Roman poet Horace stared solemnly from my open book, dwelling on wine's power to loosen a person. Omnipotent, omnipresent. And yet, over all these years, somehow my dad was always able to pull back just short of unravelling fully. Maybe his thread was golden from the good he had done, like that scene with the Fates in Disney's *Hercules*:

Clotho: 'What's the matter with these scissors?'

Atropos: 'The thread won't cut!'

My brother started emailing me:

> *Re: (No subject)*
>
> Sun 24 May 2015 6:28 PM
>
> *Dad is being moody again what should I do the food is burning and mum is out*

My final exams began the next morning. My head wasn't in the game.

Danny's emails escalated:

> *Re:*
>
> Thu 28 May 2015 8:31 AM
>
> *The house is a disgrace today and everything keeps going missing here. Dad came home drunk again last night and mum didn't do anything again so now I am moaning because he has my belt in the gym bag. I hope he crashes on the motorway today.*
> *From Dan xxx*
> *I am so stressed.*

If I didn't know how to cope with it, what chance did Danny have? He had the mind of a young child, disguised in an adult's body. I didn't know what to say to him anymore. Sometimes I didn't reply.

~

I was in my room when my phone buzzed. A course-mate was stressed about the next day's literature exam. We texted back and forth. I mentioned my dad's latest disappearance. He was still missing. She told me to come to hers. She said we'd cheer each other up. I resisted, she insisted, off I went.

When I got there, the course-mate was sobbing. She didn't stop. I took her for pasta on George Street. I chose a booth where her tears wouldn't dilute other diners' evenings. I walked her home, photocopied my notes for her, then headed back to my room. The exam was fine, unmemorable. As in, I literally can't remember it.

I realised I was sad more than I was happy. I booked a slot with a uni counsellor. She surveyed my responses to her questionnaire, noting no suicidal thoughts, just bouts of distress, anxiety, and panic. I laid out the situation for her. The violence in our family, my fears and compulsions when it came to going back.

'Your composure, it baffles me,' she said. 'Most people would cry or shout in your circumstances.'

I tried to explain that this was just how it was for us. 'I do cry sometimes in my room,' I offered.

She advised me to hold off processing what was happening, in case it 'unravelled' me.

'You should focus on your exams for now,' she concluded.

I tried, for a while.

~

One night in early June, just before bed, I had a text from Lisa. She said her mum had been suffering some pain and was going in for tests. *We're not using the c word*, she wrote. I woke up to another text. A doctor had said her mum had days to live. From decades to days, in minutes. The family was flying over to say goodbye. The cancer was everywhere. I leapt out of bed and called my own mum. She picked up. I was hysterical, unable to speak.

'Sophie, talk to me,' she shouted over my tears. 'Sophie? Sophie!'

'It's Hazel,' I gasped, 'She's going to die.' I told her what had happened.

'Come home now,' my mum said.

Phone, keys, wallet. I grabbed sunglasses to hide my eyes and ran to catch the next train. That month of horror was hot. T-shirt and shorts weather. We sat together in the lurid sunshine and drank tea on my family's decking. I posted a photo captioned *Beautiful people*.

'This is a wake-up call for your father,' my mum declared as she took our mugs inside. He was always the main character.

I got a train back to Oxford the night before my next exam. I bumped into my despairing course-mate on St Giles. She was dry-faced this time. She asked how I was. I said I had better get on.

I decided all I wanted from the remaining exams was to enjoy them. Before each one, I went for breakfast alone at a posh hotel-brasserie a few doors down from Exam Schools. I shuffled my notes over scrambled eggs and coffee. I must have amused guests, kitted out in *sub fusc*, the required academic dress: black gown, white blouse, ribbon, skirt, tights. The carnation pinned to my chest turned from white to pink to red, signalling the nearness of the end. All the while I smiled like some kind of lunatic.

Danny's emails continued:

Re:

Mon 1 June 2015 5:27 PM

I have been to the oaks today working in the rain dead heading the old leaves on the plants. I saw my girlfriend yesterday in youth club who is married to me now and I am telling the truth here because she had a ring on her finger and I did. Al was doing my head in last night by sulking and looking at me but I was a grown up I ignored him and said he is a fool.
From Dan.

Re: (No subject)

Wed 3 June 2015 5:41 PM

Everything is missing in the house but it will get found in the end because it is not very far.

I emailed my brother the next day:

Thu 4 June 2015 12:27 PM

You're absolutely right about the things in the house. They'll all be there somewhere.

on y va

My exams ended, but I couldn't face moving back to Cardiff right away. I held it off as long as I could, lingering in college accommodation. One dawn I climbed through a window onto the roof and sat watching the dawn break behind Merton Cathedral, silhouetted against burning streaks of sunrise. I drove home for Bee then took her back to Oxford in my little blue Citroen. We picked strawberries and ate Thai food across summery days, denying, or at least delaying, reality.

When I did go back, it was to eleven months of turmoil. I put my things in that dead-end terrace four roads over from our family's house. I had signed the paperwork by then, against my will. I didn't always sleep there, though. I never knew where an evening would take me. What I did come to know is that my dad and I would never truly be friends again.

I was due to graduate in July. Given how unstable my dad was by then, I was adamant that I'd go by myself. Danny had similar concerns:

Re: (No subject)

Sun 26 Jul 2015 5:03 PM

Dad will be a embarrassment in the ceremony like he normally is a embarrassment

Usually I responded patiently to my brother's emails, all smiley faces and cheery encouragement, but that evening before my graduation

I was thrumming with panic. I snapped:

Sun 26 Jul 2015 5:04 PM

Danny can you just shut up for once

I set off early the next day, eventually letting Bee and our parents follow behind with Grandma. It was nice, to my surprise. Bee and our dad surprised me with a bouquet of gigantic sunflowers. He drank, of course, but by the time they left there had been no incidents. I celebrated by going for tea with a Scouse friend and her family at the local Spoons.

Mon 27 Jul 2015 4:45 PM

Hope your graduation ceremony goes well and nothing ruins it.
How is dad behaving.
Love you From Dan

As a family, we rollercoastered between love, fury, panic, joy. Everything was felt deeply and quickly. Nothing lasted, not even anger. A few days after graduation, I took my siblings on a day-trip to Hay-on-Wye. The sun beamed at us. We bookshop-hopped and had lunch at The Blue Boar, laughing with and at each other. I spent much of that summer running and reading and writing, in other words, finding any and every possible means of escape.

Two of our five cats moved into the dead-end terrace, and two others took it upon themselves to relocate to various neighbours' houses. Meanwhile, Danny went into respite more and more.

Re: (No subject)

Thu 13 Aug 2015 9:20 PM

It is better than home here it is peaceful and quiet. I do miss the family and you but I am settling in here. I am watching the news I have been to visionmade today.
Miss you Dan xxx

Thu 13 Aug 2015 9:31 PM

I am here again because of dad's drinking behaviour in squash and work.

Sun 16 Aug 2015 11:21 AM

I am a bit stressed about things at the moment about what dad's behaviour is going to be like when I go back home on Tuesday from new road ... I felt sorry for this homeless man when we went Albany Road so I gave him 10p to make him happy.

Sat 22 Aug 2015 7:58 PM

Hi it is dan
Dad has been wasting his money all day on food, drink and a 50 pounds squash racket from John Lewis.
I wish I wasn't alive and I wish I didn't live in my house with not a proper family. So I wish had a proper father and proper mum because I don't want to live anymore I would rather throw myself off a bridge or go into the river Taff.
This is the end of me
Dan

I wrote back with soothing replies. Sometimes I rang, or took him for hot chocolate. He joined me and my friends for a meal at The Clink, where he bonded with the staff and was given a book of poetry. He read some pages aloud at the table. I tried to be a proper sister, even if I didn't believe we were a proper family anymore.

~

That month, August, I noticed injustice for the first time and found that I cared about that, too. The news brought images of a toddler washed up dead on a beach. Alan Kurdi, drowned in his little red T-shirt. His family had escaped Syria, and now he lay on the shore of Turkey. Just a baby. I had holidayed there once.

A refugee camp in Calais came onto my Facebook feed. Calais, the port I had been waved through, back and forth, since I was a baby. I posted a call-out for clothes, blankets, cans, anything I could take there. Heaps of donations piled up in my living room. My next-door neighbours helped me sift through it. My parents had always laughed at do-gooders. Earnestness was mocked, deemed soft. I suppose becoming one of the do-gooders was something of a rebellion.

The day I was due to leave, I got up early and set off for Dover in my little blue Citroen, packed to the brim with donations. I had a backing track of six missed calls from my parents. The tabloids had portrayed the camp as unsafe: a site of violence, angst, power plays. Even if it were the case, our family's house had me well prepared.

My brother was scared of me being there. He fired off some ugly emails, then this:

Re: (No subject)

Tue 1 Sep 2015 3:26 PM

I am sorry for saying mean things to you about your trip to France. I feel guilty for being selfish and mean to you. But I am still your brother and friend. I just get carried away with this kind of charity stuff people do sometimes I am a nice person and a mean person but

accidents happen when you get moody and then you turn happy in the end. You are still my sister and my friend we are part of our family and should not argue because we are friends.
Dan

Tue 1 Sept 2015 3:41 PM

Yes, I am your friend and I count you as one of my closest friends too. It is wrong to think that other people who have fewer friends in life do not deserve help to survive. We have to be supportive, especially to those who aren't lucky enough to have families and friends who can look after them. I'm not giving away your things or anything that is important to the old owners, these are only spare things that are no longer needed here but will be very useful to people without homes. I hope that you understand better now.
Sophie

I spent the first night at our French house before heading back towards Calais the next morning. I turned off the highway in Pas-de-Calais and slipped below a grey bridge, then parked up outside a warehouse. A volunteer knocked on the car window and smiled, introducing himself. His name was Riaz, and he grew up in Pakistan. He took me around the camp, smiling and shaking hands with everyone we passed.

We stopped for food in a carpeted tent known as The Afghan Kitchen. I tried 'ladies' fingers', okra, for the first time. Kind men gave me chicken and rice, refusing to take my euros. Riaz took me to Jungle Books, the refugee camp's makeshift library. There was a sign:

Read, write, talk. Art, music, play. Everyone welcome.

The sun shone with the dregs of summer. Up the hill, I played with Abba, a toddler in a second-hand *Surfers' Paradise* T-shirt. I tried to shake the image of baby Alan on the beach. Abba clamoured for my attention as he set sail his paper boat on a puddle. It floated for a few seconds then crumpled and sank. His smile wobbled. I don't remember how I reacted.

By the end of the day, Riaz was calling me his sister. We stayed friends for years, then lost touch when I deleted Facebook. I regret that. Many of the people I met were fleeing conflict and persecution across arbitrary borders. I drove back to our French house, our second home. A spare home. A quarter of an hour into my drive there, I realised I was supposed to have checked if anyone was stowed in the car. I pulled over, horrified that I cared. We had five extra beds lying empty.

The next day was as opposite as could be. Gloomy clouds loomed overhead, then rain bucketed down over the camp. Potholes flooded. People ran to take cover in leaking tents. I pulled up my hood and tried to help monitor the food queue. It felt inhumane to stand here and tell hungry people not to cut the line. I had never been denied a thing.

I headed back to Cardiff humming with outrage and righteousness. I started looking at supermarket shelves with something like disgust. Those injustices were worse than our own, something worthier of my focus. I tried to rise above my dad's drinking. That is, I tried to ignore it.

~

My Journalism MA got underway. I presented, to myself and others, a carefreeness. I suppose it was a fuller answer to my philosophy tutor Ursula's question five years earlier: is it possible to lie to yourself? My truth was selective, full of holes.

It was fair to say I enjoyed the tasks and frenzied atmosphere of our student newsroom. I excelled in my course, hardened by years of practice. I had a resilience coupled with a fuck-it-why-not that worked pretty well for reporting. Nothing threw me. I hosted parties at the dead-end terrace and went on impromptu trips. I didn't sleep much. I drank a fair bit.

I spent as little time as possible in the dead-end terrace. I learned of Banksy's pop-up Dismaland, for instance, and scrabbled for a ticket. One cold weeknight I went to Weston-super-Mare. *Keep an eye on your longings*, whispered a piece of graffiti there.

'PLANNING FOR THE FUTURE IS ESCAPISM,' announced Banksy's loudspeaker while I dangled over Dismaland on the Ferris wheel.

In two weeks, my dad and I were due to run the Cardiff Half. 4 October 2015. It'd be a stretch to describe our lifestyles as athletic at this point. He was either absent or smashed. I was hardly much better, though I toyed with the idea of training. One night I went over to our family's house to wait for him to get back from work, or rather to get home from the pretence of work. He and I had agreed to go for a run together. He was very late home from work, and very drunk.

He laughed at seeing me waiting in my vest and leggings, his eyes bloodshot.

'C'mon then, let's hit the road,' he said. '*On y va.*'

I didn't move. 'You can't. You're hammered.'

He shook his head and went first, stumbling down our drive in his baggy shorts and ripped rugby jersey. I watched, then set off, chest pounding before we had even got started.

I overtook him and waited at the corner of Dan-y-Coed Road, flinching as he tripped over his feet and scudded across the pavement. Gashes tore open his knees. I went on, hoping he'd turn back. He huffed up Bettws-y-Coed Road while blood dripped down his legs.

Cars passed. No one we knew, I prayed. Another loud slap as his body hit the tarmac again. I stopped, my heart pounding, as he lay there, crimson now smeared across his palms, wrists, chin. This was my fault, I thought. I said nothing. He was smirking. Why did we have to be like this?

It used to be that he was forever ahead, staying just above my pace to challenge me, to make me a better runner. He was the one who waited patiently. Like that time I begged to join the weekly five-miler with the men on our street. I lagged from the get-go, but my dad jogged on the spot and buoyed me up Penylan Hill even when the rest of them were well out of sight.

In the half marathon itself he was faster than me. He so often drew on miraculous inner resources. I don't know how he did it. We posed with our medals for a photo. I posted it on Facebook.

There was no planning, no escaping. Banksy knew what he was talking about. Over and over, my mum said she was leaving him. Each week, she stayed. The two of them let themselves into the dead-end terrace, theoretically my home, whenever they liked, turning up unannounced at any hour. For me, it was just another place to feel cornered. I ended up going back and forth between there and our family's house, sleeping wherever felt less angsty in the given moment. It wasn't much of a strategy, I admit.

The leaves turned a roaring red that month. One evening I was at our family's house with Bee and Milno, our friend from three doors up. We were chatting over tea, messing around, when my mum had one of those calls from him. The slurring sort that warned us we didn't have long to get out. Most importantly, to get Danny away, before he could lash out and mayhem would ensue. Disaster was a very real possibility.

For me and Bee, our dad's drinking could be unnerving, even alarming. Danny's learning difficulties and autism meant all of this was amplified for him. His bewilderment and fury were getting harder and harder to handle. We kept telling social services that we were at crisis point. Their response seemed to be to wait for the crisis.

Our friend Milno watched, upset, as we darted about, bundling the things we needed for a night elsewhere. Pyjamas, chargers, Danny's meds. I'm not exactly sure why I went with them. Solidarity? Safety in numbers? Keeping them where I could see them? There is a lot from this period that seems strange to me now, but I know I never felt safe in the dead-end terrace. It's not that my dad had ever physically hurt me, but in my head this always came with a ... *yet*. His slamming and throwing and cursing meant the possibility never felt far-fetched. He had a key.

'Where are you thinking?' I asked as my mum reversed fast off the drive.

'My brother's,' she replied. She glanced at Danny. 'Just for tonight.'

It had been a struggle to get Danny into the car. His fists were still scrunched in anxiety. No one spoke. We were waiting for the explosion. We didn't make it to her brother's. Danny opened the car door just before the M4. Our mum changed course. To Grandma's, around the corner, where we were received with a talking-to that 'this really couldn't continue.' Spoiler: it could, and did, for years.

~

My dad was right when he used to say I won first prize in the lottery of life. For me, that prize was a predisposition towards joy. I was geared to have a good time. Laughter, fun. Despite the chaos, I felt upbeat among Cardiff's vivid parks, unhurried river, silvery buildings, rippling coast, misty hills, lilting people.

I started seeing the man I would marry. I vaguely knew him from Oxford, and he was doing a project in Cardiff. We went for dinners in town and talked about books, films, places. It felt like a space to breathe, somewhere I could feign not being the sort of person who has to haul loved ones out of disorder twice, thrice weekly. I didn't mention the dysfunction for a few months, not until I had to. At first I could almost, not quite, tune out of the background noise just beyond our meals together. Meanwhile, the hum of violence got worse, threatening to topple into emergencies.

Family life started to feel like one long heavy night spent anticipating a painfully early start. On the more difficult days I sleepwalked through wakeful hours fitfully, constantly on the alert, panicking that I had missed cues to get moving. Any rustle was unnerving, every creak a threat. I was constantly jumpy, imagining the alarm was about to go off. My mind strained under the constant wait for the alarm, my mum's ringtone, blaring with the call we all dreaded. He was drunk again. Go, go, go.

Bee and I did make a failed attempt to get away from it all. She was sixteen, soon to sit her GCSEs. We stayed with my friends, pretending they were sleepovers, with lots of tea and takeaways. I finished assignments cross-legged on Milno's pull-out sofa. We slept a night or two in Lisa's brother's old room. Her mum had outlived the doctors' prognosis of days but she was very ill. At the kitchen table, she sipped hot water while I had a cuppa.

'You and Lisa will always look out for each other,' she said.

'Of course,' I smiled. 'I know we will.'

My mum was ringing and emailing. She demanded to know why I was keeping her daughter away from her, as if my sister's exhaustion and trauma came as a surprise to her. She reminded me I was not Bee's mother. I sent her a tense email after one of these calls.

Re: .

Fri 18 Dec 2015 3:55 PM

Your whole approach to that call was incredible – how was it remotely fair of you (1) to accuse me of "keeping" Bee here after how she was treated at home (2) suggest the family's mess is in any way my fault??? I'm trying not to be angry but it's very difficult.

Her response? Same as it ever was. Hesitation, repetition, deviation.

Fri 18 Dec 2015 4:01 PM

I haven't said it's your fault. I'm trying to understand why Bee won't come home, why I am the one in the wrong and why you are angry? Yes I said I was leaving your father but he went willingly to the GP yesterday with me and I sat there and listened to the sadness and despair that he felt and the abhorration of his weakness in his addiction. He went for lots of tests today. He has a massive problem with addiction. Our family is in despair and the GP is aware of this. We can go to family therapy and we must talk. I was appalled also at how much shit Bee has to deal with and I am completely ashamed that I couldn't protect her. Life is difficult.

On Christmas Eve, I went to The Three Arches with my friends. It was our school's tradition. I was just getting into the swing of it when I got a call an hour or so in.

'I'm taking Danny to Grandma's,' my mum said. 'Your sister is home alone.'

'Where's our dad?'

'Who knows, he came back pissed. Gone out again. Drinking away more of our money probably.'

I said flustered goodbyes to my friends and put on my coat. I walked fast, then started to run down Rhydypenau Road. In the lamplight I saw a figure stumbling towards me, pub-wards. I barely slowed. We looked at each other, my dad and I, and neither of us said a word. What was the point? I went home and watched a festive feel-good film with Bee. My friends texted when he arrived at The Three Arches ten minutes later. The next morning I drove the three of us to Grandma's. It was another Christmas to forget. When one of you is a drinker, special occasions signal days to dread in particular.

The new year brought new lows, though Bee and I tried to see the beauty. We went up Caerphilly Mountain to take in a nice sunset. I went back and forth to London. My mum continued emailing from a few roads away. One was so good I screenshotted it. I don't know where she got hold of the Larkin quotes.

(no subject)

Tue 26 Jan 2016. 1:54 PM

They (we) fuck you up your mum and dad
They may not mean to but they (we) do

*They (we) fill you with the faults they (we) had
and add some extra (alcohol-panic) just for you .... Please if you can
find peace in your troubled mind will you phone him and meet up
with him. Today. He wants to make it up to you and be your friend.*

My troubled mind. I was the problem, you see.

Then it was February, its brevity a blessing. Dusk. I was in the dead-end terrace, sitting with friends on the rug when my phone lit up.

'Come quickly,' my mum said, as she often did. This time, though, she sounded all the more breathless. 'I need you to take Danny.'

I got there in minutes. My sister's friend was waiting on the doorstep.

'Your dad—'. She couldn't speak.

I stepped inside. My mum was on the phone in the front room, bent over my dad, who was swaying on the arm of the settee. He was hardly conscious, drunk of course, clutching his shoulder. Stuck into it was the black handle of a kitchen knife. I didn't see the blade. Blood stained his white shirt.

I went to find my brother. His eyes were darting around, unable to focus, wide and afraid. His hands were shaking.

'Hey DB, shall we pop out for a bit,' I said, taking his arm.

I drove us to Grandma's, five minutes around the corner, but she didn't answer the door. It was almost half six, past her bedtime. I called Lisa to say we were coming to hers, also only a few roads away. My mum rang again as I was turning the car around. I put her on speakerphone.

'You need to come back,' she said. '*Heddlu*.' Police. She used the Welsh to avoid panicking Danny. I took us back, picking my lip until it bled.

I saw the vans before he did. Police, all over our street. There must have been at least six, seven of them. Paramedics had taken our dad to hospital. Danny's hands scrambled, reaching for the door handles. His body was clenched with fear.

'I'm not in trouble, am I, Soph?' His voice trembled.

'No, no, you're alright,' I switched off the engine. 'Let's put the kettle on.'

I placed him in front of the TV while my mum pleaded with the police officers. She had convinced them to put the long-barrelled weapons and ballistic helmets back in their vehicles. They needed to take Danny into custody, they said, given the situation. It had been the two of them in the kitchen. Our dad must have been drunkenly gutting his fish. I agreed to be the appropriate adult, officially taking up the role I had held all my life.

'Daniel,' one of the officers said, 'As a result of the incident that occurred earlier with your dad I am now arresting you on suspicion of Section 18 Assault. You do not have to say anything, but it may harm your defence if you do not mention when questioned something which you later rely on in court. Anything you do say may be given in evidence.'

'Go on, DB,' I nodded brightly at my brother.

Danny gave a thumbs-up and said, 'Okay.'

We climbed into one of the police vans. We made small talk. One of the officers said he lived in Barry. We spoke about our Sunday routine, keeping the tone chipper. Twenty minutes later we were at the station down Cardiff Bay. A young guy, our age-ish, was being released.

'Nah, love, you look way too nice to be here,' he called across to me. 'Let her go,' he yelled as he buckled the belt he had been handed back. I smiled a sheepish thanks.

They took Danny's things and put us in a cell. We sat side by side on the hard bench and played hangman in the notebook that was always in my coat pocket. It was the journalist in me. At some point a pair of tray dinners were slid in for us. I don't recall what was on the menu.

What I remember most is begging the staff to let me give Danny his epilepsy meds, which were among the things they had taken off us. He needed them twice a day to ward off fits. They said no, not yet, they needed to be checked.

'He'll have a fit without them. Please,' I whispered, trying not to let him hear. 'Stress already puts him at serious risk.'

They shrugged. 'You'll have to wait for the medic's verdict.'

I lay knotted with tension on the floor, my coat as a pillow. I watched Danny sleeping. There was no darkness and no natural light, just white strobes leaking in from the corridor. Despite it all, he looked peaceful. I took a photo. I had been allowed to keep my phone on a technicality: I wasn't the one being imprisoned. I couldn't reach anyone, in any case, thanks to the block on signal.

The next day, we ate breakfast, then lunch. Again I couldn't tell you what. I don't know how we passed all that time. More games in my notebook, I suppose. At one point I asked if I could get a snack and a magazine from the newsagents down the road. They couldn't say no.

I told Danny I'd be back as quickly as I could. I hurried outside and was struck by all the daylight. Fresh air. Space. It felt so strange, and it had been less than twenty-four hours. Imagine a lifetime, I thought to myself.

With my few minutes of 3G, I looked up the max penalty for Section 18 assault. Life imprisonment. For my disabled brother, whose mental age was eight, this was a death sentence. I ran down the steps and jumped in shock. Our dad was loitering there. Extremely drunk. This station was something of a home from home for him by now.

'How's Danny?' he said, his face pinched tight.

I said nothing, picking up my pace towards the newsagents. He followed me, repeating the question over and over as I walked, 'How's Danny?' As I grabbed a Bounty, 'How's Danny?', as I flung over coins at the till, 'How's Danny?' As I hurried back to the station, 'How's Danny?'

I asked the receptionist if I could please go back into the jail, where I'd be safe. She said I'd have to wait. My dad lurched next to me, slurring this latest refrain of his, 'How's Danny?'

I stood stock still, silent, staring at the door into where Danny was being held. The whole waiting room watched us. I felt like I was playing a character in a TV drama. The staff finally realised something was up and took me through. I left my dad there without a backwards glance.

This was all his doing. He knew it, I knew it. Everyone should have known it. And yet here we were inside, there he was outside. Not a sorry in sight, though he made for a very sorry sight.

The police had asked my mum if she wanted to give them a statement about my dad's behaviour. Eventually she did, then refused to sign it. There was nothing any of us could do.

Later that day, I sat in the waiting area while Danny went in for questioning. My little brother had never looked so small. I prayed to a god I didn't believe in that they'd release him on bail. I sat tapping my leg, picking my lips.

Sometime later, who knows how long, I spotted Danny shuffling out and gasped in relief. He was clutching some papers. I still have his charge sheet all these years later. My brother's childlike handwriting, all giant trembly unjoined letters, in the signature box. Dyspraxia was one of the many conditions that hampered his ability to get by in this society. It was so unfair, the way disabilities congregated in him.

We were allowed to go home. I went straight up to Bee's room. She had gone mute, my mum said. Milno came round, and I drove the three of us to the new Starbucks Drive-Thru in Cardiff Bay. She still didn't speak for a while, then cheered up over a Frappuccino. I rang my boyfriend, Ash, and had to explain that I hadn't answered his texts because I was in a prison cell. It was then that I let him behind the scenes of what my family was really like.

My dad wasn't around that night. I knew then that there could be no 'wake-up call', even if he did parrot the right lines to placate my mum when needed. I understood the stark reality that he did not intend to stop drinking. If he felt any guilt, he hid it well. The dissonance made me sick.

I mean, really sick. Not that you'd have realised it on seeing me around this time. The next morning, after leaving the jail cell, I was back in journalism class, acting as editor-in-chief at the student newspaper. I was breezy, competent, smiling, fine on the surface. Fine on the surface. And yet, to put it bluntly, inside I was quietly going a little bit mad.

~

Spring eased in, and I posted photos of cherry blossom, blue skies, Welsh cakes, the rockpool waterfalls at Monk Nash. I scroll through these images, archived in my Instagram. They weren't lies, my online snapshots of pleasure in these moments. My cheerfulness wasn't a pretence.

Life was mercurial, untethering. I was happy and sad and all the things in between. My mind misted more and more, dazed by the thick haze of relentless instability. I had experienced total loss of control for so long, how fitting that I'd also slightly lose my head. I felt an ongoing impulse to flee. By summer I would, but that spring I was suffocating.

My mum had my dad move in with me. Danny's bail conditions meant he and our dad could no longer live in the same house. Each night, I woke in sweats of terror. This continued throughout my twenties. He stumbled home later and later. I found a shirt soaked in vomit on the hallway floor. This was a change. I had never known him to throw up. It must have been a rager. I put it in the washing machine. I was twenty-two. It was the longest year of my life, and easily the worst.

He could be kind one minute, belligerent the next. I began to tiptoe around the latter. Any critical comments might set him off. I managed the situation by mirroring him. When he was kind, I was warm. When he was hostile, I was cold. We could be mates over breakfast and enemies by midday.

Our mornings were the same but different. Still his Radio 4, still his Taylor's coffee. We no longer discussed the Ultimate Question. Perhaps neither of us cared, at that point, what it was all about. Our routine had soured.

In late March 2016, we went on our last trip together. Him, me, and Bee. To our home in northern France, where our travels began. To end at the beginning.

There was something new in our town, or would I just not have noticed it before? A poster, taped to a brick wall. A black and white photo of a young boy in a puffer jacket. Behind him, tents. Below him, white text:

Aprés 3000kms parcourus ... je reste un enfant...
(After travelling 3000km ... I'm still a child...)

I had been back to the Calais camp that December just gone. It was freezing, wet, depressing. We took over blankets and winter-wear. I didn't really know where to go from there. There was too much going on in my brain.

On this last visit to France with my dad, we got croissants and p.a.c.s from Monsieur Grémont. We were blown about on Le Crotoy. We ate moules-frites at Les Canotiers. Our dad disappeared for a few hours one evening, leaving me and Bee at home, hungry, wondering where he was. He returned staggering, slurring. We didn't expect anything else. This was what happened. We had to take the bad with the good. I was snarky, threatening to drive back to Wales without him. We got pizza. I read my book.

~

A few weeks later, Grandma came over to the dead-end terrace unannounced and found me crouched hyperventilating in the kitchen. She drove me back to hers, two roads away, and watched me with concern until my sobs eased.

'What can I do to help you?' she asked, spreading her hands. I said nothing and shook my head. I shouldn't have shown I was flustered. It wasn't my style.

It felt like I was the only one who could see the person we loved was dying. I could read him better than I could read myself. He would never give up drinking. It would kill him, maybe us too. I knew this, though I'd never say it to his face. I feared that if I acted to him like it was bound to happen, I'd be playing a role in making it so.

My MA chugged on. I interviewed the First Minister in a deli. I did a feature on Welsh-language classes at the local refugee centre. I went to events like 'Reporting Family Proceedings'. That last one was a bit close to home. May and June brought more exams. I barely remember revising. Instead, I sent off job applications to anyone and everyone in London. I needed to leave. I said yes, please, to the first HR person to give me a shot. How soon could I start?

One day I left the exam hall and saw my phone screen was full of missed calls. I rang back in the car park and learned my dad had been arrested again. Drink-driving. The difference was there'd be a trial this time. He could be imprisoned.

'Thank god,' I said, perched on the kerb.

It was a neighbour who had made the call to the police. My mum had been screaming at our dad out on the street again after one of the many times he had driven home in his Mercedes while totally off his face. He was back at the wheel, fumbling, keys in the ignition, when the police van arrived. The timing was everything.

He had been getting away with this crime for years. He was above the law, he thought. Rules weren't for men like him, right? I realise now he easily could have killed someone on the roads. Sometimes he was so drunk he could barely walk. I feel like I was complicit, keeping his secret for him. For us? Tribalism can be confusing. Cowardly.

I finished my last exam on a Friday in June and deferred my dissertation. I knew I could get a Distinction but didn't care enough to attempt it at the time. I needed a city of my own, and money that was mine. The next day, that Saturday, I left Cardiff and moved into a grimy sublet down an alley off Camden High Street. The staircase was filthy. The windows had bars. Distance from Cardiff: 130 miles. Freedom, at last?

complete chaos and disaster

On my first night in London, I had dinner with Ash. He lived near Brixton and was the main reason I had moved to the city. I was very in love with him but kept my cards close to my chest. I assumed I'd probably lose him too. We ate in the basement of a quiet, white-washed Greek taverna. Family run, simple stuff. After our meal, Ash said he'd leave me to my unpacking. We hugged on the street and he took the Northern line back to his flat south of the river. I woke alone to an empty Sunday.

On Monday I began as an in-house journalist for a shiny American company. My job was to source great photography, write words to go with it, and get it into newspapers. Was I excited? Possibly, in a nervous energy sort of way.

It was an office in London Bridge, open plan and fluro-lit. On Wednesdays we had free breakfasts and free massages. On Fridays we had free lunches. I made friends, sort of, with all the middle-aged ex-Fleet Street men around me. For most of that time, I was the only woman in the room. Sometimes there were sexist jokes. My manager apologised, grimacing behind his beard, for the 'locker room talk'. I laughed, thinking it was the norm. Wasn't it?

The men went en masse to the pub on Friday afternoons. I wasn't invited, thankfully. I waved them off and soaked up the quiet. I liked the absence of people spinning on chairs and barking down phones.

A week or so into my time in London, the referendum took place, as promised in the previous summer's election. That felt like a lifetime ago. My friends and I loosely followed the build-up, complacent that everyone thought like we did: obviously we shouldn't cut ourselves off from Europe. I popped in to vote before work and was rewarded with a blue sticker shouting *I'M IN*. I still have it.

That night, some of my uni friends had a party in their airy flat on Finchley Road. We slouched on plush sofas, tipsy and inattentive. We pored over photos of a mate's new place. We discussed another's latest girlfriend. I didn't stay up for the results, only waking to the news that we'd be leaving the EU. The polls had been wrong again. It was an era of unpredictability.

A few hours later, I arrived at the office, where colleagues stood in solemn shock around the flatscreen TVs. My manager couldn't take it. He walked out and didn't come back that day. The right-wing guy resigned. I saw that Wales was majority-Leave. I felt a rip in my chest, as if suddenly estranged from somewhere I felt had changed there and then. It felt like a self-inflicted wound, egged on by the lies of self-serving men.

I had been naive, though so had everyone else. At twenty-two, I had no idea about the depths of Welsh Brexit voters' sense of betrayal, of isolation. I had dipped my toes into injustice overseas, but was yet to learn about the desperation on my doorstep.

I called my mum at lunchtime. It wouldn't actually happen, would it? It couldn't, could it? We reassured ourselves that we wouldn't be cut adrift. If only we were in our French house, we thought, then we'd feel less disorientated. It was the place where I had taken my first steps, had my first period, first had sex.

~

It was a summer of attempted ruptures. My mum finally tried to leave my dad, who was worse than ever, though it would be five more years before she pressed ahead with it. She forwarded me the letter her lawyer had sent. I read it at work. An extract:

We are instructed that on 18 July 2016 the police were called to [redacted] where our client is residing. You were in the property and you were drunk and argumentative. Danny was particularly upset and agitated about seeing you in this state. Due to your abusive nature towards our client and Danny the police had to be involved on no less than three occasions. This is the culmination of many years of emotional abuse you have subjected our client to when drunk. Your difficulty with alcohol over recent times has had a detrimental impact upon our client's well-being and also the well-being of the children and the wider family. This will no longer be tolerated by our client.

I replied to her on my lunch-break:

Wed 20 Jul 2016 12:31 PM

I've just read it, that's good. Well done Mum.x

She wrote back within two minutes:

Wed 20 Jul 2016 12:33 PM

I am v scared now. I was at [redacted] about an hour ago and he turned up but didn't see nor speak to me. I hope he doesn't kill me.

I messaged again:

Wed 20 Jul 2016 12:36 PM

I'm scared too, I'd leave if I were you. I've asked Bee to come to London.

Half an hour later, I had an email from my dad. He forwarded the letter sent by the lawyer, and added thirteen words just for me. Words I would never unsee:

Wed 20 Jul 2016 1:05 PM

So there we go. It's all over now. Expect complete chaos and disaster.

Complete chaos and disaster. Chaos and disaster. Disaster. His warning palpitated. I was already frightened that he might kill us, out of spite, out of rage that he was no longer in charge. Sometimes it felt like he was slipping into a world of self-destruction and taking us with him. I pressed plane mode and fed my phone to my back pocket to digest.

I returned to my ergonomic chair, adjustable desk, widescreens, and trivial tasks I could do in my sleep. I smiled at the men's jokes. I asked if anyone would like a tea. I replied to emails with many thanks and best wishes. At a respectable 5:05 pm, I hurried down the station steps into the city's arteries. Northern line. I kept my eyes fixed on my feet, a way to be invisible.

Tunnel lights flared every few seconds. Northbound to where the black lines cut diagonally and met like the spear of a needle. Pale blue-purple tiles, black letters.

CAMDEN TOWN

I resurfaced and put in headphones without bothering to turn on music on the escalator. It was a last-ditch defence against the strangers who bayed and brushed against me each day. This happened without fail on my eight-minute walk up and down the high street. I did not dress for attention. Loose tops, flat shoes, no make-up. I never knew why this happened to me.

Perhaps I smiled too readily. Perhaps I looked like easy prey. Perhaps angst had a scent that radiated when I was young and afraid. Or perhaps, I wonder now, it was nothing to do with me and everything to do with them. Their greed, their hunger for power. If pursued these days I walk fast, purposeful, to signal I exist for more than their taking. Back then I was just so done with it all.

That first month in London, my mind jittered constantly with scenes of appeals, prison visits, consequences. I jumped at any noise. Sirens blared at all hours, in my days and in my dreams. I functioned on autopilot. Even 130 miles away, I still hadn't escaped.

My mum rang one day on my lunch-break. She said my brother's trial, *Regina v Danny*, was over. And he was free, well, free as he ever could be. The judge had an autistic child. She understood he was no criminal, just a scared and confused kid. My knees gave way. Danny moved into the dead-end terrace, where he was slightly safer at least. My dad's trial was uneventful. No prison time, just a fine and a driving ban for a while. Consequences, of sorts.

~

August soared in with chords of sublime promise. I moved in with Ash for a few months while his brother was abroad. I fell into more of a routine and slept a bit better at night. I saw my first parakeet on Stockwell Crescent. Life became milder, happier.

My dad kept writing to me, but I rarely replied. Behind his words he pleaded for my forgiveness, for my friendship:

Re: certainty

Sat 10 Sep 2016 4:00 PM

Things haven't been particularly good recently but there is still a long way to go. It will all come good in the end. That is certain.

Re: New Job

Mon 31 Oct 2016 7:50 PM

My big deal still isn't finished. I worked like a dog on it yesterday and into the early hours this morning. I am so tired. Are you OK? How is the money going? If you need any help, just let me know ... Love you old mate. Dad

In autumn, I went home for a weekend. Yes, Cardiff was 'home' even then. I know this because I was still calling it that on Instagram over the years until then:

Home sooooooooon (May, 2015)

Homeward bound (Aug, 2015)

Light at the end of the Severn tunnel. HOME 🐿 (Apr, 2016)

#Home is tea & olives & new canvases (Sept, 2016)

That September trip was the last time I called Cardiff 'home'.

I messaged Nan to ask if Bee and I could come to Barry for a cup of tea. I didn't want to see my dad, wherever he was. He wasn't living with our family at that point. I think he was sleeping on a mate's settee. *Please don't tell him I'm here*, I texted Nan, for the avoidance of doubt.

We got to Barry, let ourselves in, hugged, went to kick off our— saw his shoes in our spot below the stairs. I stopped. I looked at Nan. Her face creased in pain.

'He just arrived, Soph, honest.'

I didn't believe her. There was a split second where I had to make a call: leave or stay. I couldn't go. I was more inclined to be hurt than to cause it.

I stepped into the living room and he was in the spare armchair, shoulders hunched in self-pity. Baggage at his feet. An untouched tea. Grandad stood for a moment, then returned to his chair in the far corner. I was simmering, beyond angry at being trapped again.

Nan fretted, quivering the saucers as she brought our teas. She perched on the arm of our dad's chair and tried to break the ice.

'He had to take the train, poor thing.'

No one replied. Bee and I sat very still next to each other on the spongy settee. We made stilted conversation, clenching our cups. I remember only a few things that were said. Like when Nan raised her hands, voice breaking as she begged me.

'You've *got* to make up with him,' she said. 'He's your dad.'

He sat behind her. To me, he looked like a child in the wrong who was letting another kid take the hit. To Nan, this was all on me. I was the troublemaker, disruptor of the peace, just like my mum had so often labelled me. Sometimes the accusation had a way of seeping in.

My mouth opened, then closed. Nan was emotional. She had no idea what he could be like. That would come later. I didn't know how, or whether, to tell her. He was watching me, her beloved son. I wouldn't, couldn't try to explain. It wasn't my place.

Soon afterwards, I got up, dazed by another warped expectation versus reality. I had thought it might be nice to visit our grandparents. Nothing happened predictably in our family anymore. Bee and I put on our shoes to leave. Nan grew even more distressed, insisting I gave my dad a lift back to Cardiff. I shook my head.

'You can't make him take the train!' she cried, as if public transport was beneath him.

Since the driving ban, he had relied on others to ferry him around. He treated my mum like a taxi driver. 'Woman,' he was calling her by then. The less power he had, the lower he sank. Worse, he was dragging Danny down with him. My brother began to call our mum 'woman', too. Bee and I were disgusted, but they wouldn't cut it out.

'Be-e kind, be-e kind,' our dad used to sing to us, usually after we had been sniping at each other. He had forgotten his own lyrics.

I did give him a lift home that day. Of course I did. I was a pushover. He began lecturing me on why I should be more sympathetic. He was really trying, he said. I ended up shouting at him as I drove down Port Road, furious that he was hijacking this small window of time that Bee and I had to spend together. Planning for the future is escapism, Banksy had said. Bee was seventeen and taking driving lessons. She longed for the day she could get herself out of there when needed.

There's a profound loneliness in setting boundaries with those you love. My mum and others kept trying to convince me I was wrong for putting space between me and my dad. In hindsight, I don't think Nan was lying. It was not in her nature. I do believe, now, that he just turned up. At the time I didn't, and blanked her messages for months. That was wrong of me.

~

The two years and nine months I lived in London were volatile. I went from job contract to job contract, flat to flat. I was on/off/on/off (cont.) with my parents. Even so, my mum emailed me constantly. Things like this:

Re: nothing

Thu 15 Dec 2016 3:59 PM

… Your father wants to come back to the house. He is pleading with me, saying he is having therapy anti-abuse etc. Everyone is carrying on in festive mode and all I can do is cry and protect myself in a solitary little world of painting tiles. What on earth can I do. Part of me thinks it is me who needs to leave the house. Bee can't stand me and shouts at me most of the time. Maybe I should give up the struggle, move out and rent somewhere for just me and start again. I can't fight any longer.

I was at work, preparing to hand in my notice. The rest of my team had moved on and I was running the features desk alone. It was tiring. I fired off a reply typed in frustration:

Thu 15 Dec 2016 4:16 PM

The problem is that this family has never had boundaries: our dad has stamped all over any stability for years, we (your children) have never known what the situ will be even within the next few hours – yet whatever awful thing that our dad/Danny has done this time, we're expected to forgive them unconditionally as soon as you do. It's never been a sustainable way of living. Of course Bee is losing her mind in that house.

The obvious answer is that you need to move out, with her, to somewhere which is the home for you and her only – a small private rental for six months. She'll live there til June then most likely move out of Cardiff. After that, you can do whatever you want. I assume you'd live with our dad, because you don't seem to want to divorce him. Until June, our dad should sort himself out in a separate property without imposing his massive issues on the rest of the family. I think the family house should be put up for sale asap – it has too many messed-up memories.

To me this is obviously what should happen but I know it won't, because I've wanted this to be the case for years. I can't offer much more than that, as when I've advised in the past it has been shot down. I am sympathetic, but I think there have been opportunities to sort this which have been wasted. It's not about fighting, it's about fixing.

She responded the next day, just after I had landed in Hamburg to see a friend. We were catching up over Kakao at a Christmas market.

Fri 16 Dec 2016 8:58 AM

I always take onboard your thoughts. I cannot always act upon them for reasons that are deep set. I will endeavour to make my children happy but what you must realise is that life is not simply a matter of just letting go. Behind the scenes of chaos there are issues being addressed and advice sought. I cannot sell the family house until divorce as we both own it. Bee is busy decorating her room/sanctuary. I am never knowing what she is thinking as she refuses to answer any leading questions. I have only your suggestions as to how/what she wants. I would like to know what Bee really wants to do for Xmas. Will you ask her. I am caught between many offshoots of emotions/ties and guilts. It isn't easy for you by any means but you are well away and are not responsible for the day to day juggling that I have dealings with. What are your plans?

The following evening my dad messaged:

Re: Hamburg

Sat 17 Dec 2016 9:32 PM

Hi Soph, what do you think of Hamburg? Looks like a lovely city from what I have seen on the internet. Hope you are having a great time.

I didn't reply.

Bee came to me for Christmas. We were sick of the rest of them. I made salmon for the two of us in my new rental, a Tulse Hill attic flat. My flatmate had gone home to be with her family, as had most Londoners apparently. We walked around Brockwell Park in the sunshine and greeted the few who remained in the city. In the evening we watched TV by the gas fire and scrolled our phones.

On Boxing Day I impulsively booked a coach north, where Ash was with his family. I took Bee to Victoria for her coach back to Cardiff, then headed up to the Peak District. It was freezing when I stepped off, but I felt warm being with him. I'd end up spending every Christmas there from then on.

~

In March, Bee was due to take her driving test. The night before the big day, I had a phone call. Our mum had let our dad come back, naturally, and he had returned from work very drunk, as was the norm. The cruel twist was that he had taken Bee's car keys and discarded them in Nant Fawr Woods. Then, to close with a bang, he got himself arrested again for being drunk and disorderly.

The neighbours tried to help Bee find the keys, but it was too late. She'd have to take the test in the instructor's car, which she had never driven before. Our dad was jealous, I guess, and bitter that she was about to have a freedom he no longer had. The cruelty was beyond belief.

I told Bee I'd be on the next train to Cardiff. I caught a bus towards Oval, where I'd take the Northern line to Waterloo, then Bakerloo to Paddington. As I stared into the fogged-up windows, I realised I was having a panic attack. I was freaking out about going back. I couldn't breathe.

I texted Ash, who told me to get off and instead come to his, midway along Brixton Road. I pressed the red button to stop the bus, by now crying and nauseous with guilt that I couldn't rush to my sister, to protect her. Looking after Bee was second nature to me. Ash coaxed me into helping him make veggie sushi. I fed my Instagram a neatly curated photo of sliced avocado, red pepper, and cucumber.

My dad went on to pretend it was no big deal. Nothing to see here, people. The following week he and I were supposed to be going to Oxford for the literary festival. I had bought a bunch of tickets as a birthday gift for him. One of the events was with Nicholas Parsons, the host of our old favourite radio show *Just a Minute*.

I can only assume my dad was doing one of his rare sober flashes in the pan when I bought the tickets. Talk about ambitious, well, naive. I'm not sure what I was thinking when I booked them, but I know what I was thinking when I refunded them: no freaking way. His latest antics had reminded me he was too unwell for us to feign friendship anymore.

Re: 31 March

Wed 29 Mar 2017 2:53 PM

Sophie
Looking forward to meeting up with you in Oxford on Friday. Give me a call to discuss arrangements.
Love
Fath.

Wed 29 Mar 2017 3:49 PM

Obviously I'm not doing that trip – I refunded the tickets straight after you were arrested and ruined my sister's long-awaited chance to drive independently last week. How can you expect me to pretend that you haven't let us all down repeatedly? My mental health is in pieces because of your drinking and aggression. I have to ask you very seriously not to contact me anymore.

Wed 29 Mar 2017 4:14 PM

Love you my old friend. Sorry if I have been a disappointment. I have tried pretty hard to look after you all. It's been quite tricky at times.
Can we do the Oxford trip please?
Dad

We didn't do the Oxford trip. There's a three-month gap in my inbox, so I must have held my nerve at least for a while before resuming contact.

My anger never lasted as long as I expected it to. That summer I was still sending my dad every draft I wrote, from articles to applications, trusting his editing skills if nothing else. In August 2017 I finally handed in my dissertation, in which I described him as *my number-one advisor from day one*. I got the Distinction I deserved.

By autumn, my cat Tilly and I had moved in with Ash. We watched indie films with subtitles and cooked exciting meals from recipes. I was finding that there were other ways to live. *Eang yw'r byd i bawb*, as the Welsh proverb goes. The world is wide to everyone. My world was widening, and it felt like my dad was shrinking inside it.

my daughter

I lasted another eighteen months in London, until early 2019, trying and frequently failing to distance myself from the family breakdown. There were still endless emails, constant phone calls. I took to blocking my parents at times, just to get a rest.

My life was fulfilling and I had the chance to be happy. I felt guilty for this. I loved living with Ash and Tilly. I loved my work in human rights. I loved my friends. I loved my sister. As for my dad, I loved and suffered him. Boomeranging between binges and short-lived sobriety, he was ever-present in my nightmares, even if I tried to put it to one side in the daytime.

It was a period of extreme restlessness. I changed jobs often, swapping short-term post for short-term post. I look back with shock, almost disgust, at how much I went away. Or maybe, to put it more accurately, how frantically I distracted myself. I couldn't stay still.

I travelled across Peru, where I canoed through the humming rainforest. To Budapest, where I cycled between coffee shops with Bee. Around Australia, where Ash and I met wallabies and wombats. To Kyiv, where I assisted a week-long workshop for journalists in conflict zones.

Across Jordan, where Ash and I had Petra spectacularly to ourselves at dawn. Around Palestine, where we talked with extraordinary people up and down the West Bank. To Ljubljana, where Lisa and I rowed across a glimmering Lake Bled. To the Côte d'Azur, where

I celebrated turning twenty-five. To Glasgow, where Ash and I devoured the city's food scene.

Around Tunisia, where I explored Roman ruins. To Istanbul, where I surprised Ash with a birthday dinner in a Bosphorus lighthouse. Back to Hamburg, where I went for icy morning runs along the Elbe. Around Argentina, where I hiked glaciers and waterfalls. To New York City, where I sweated at Russian and Turkish baths and went to jazz bars.

All this, in just two years. Eeesh. In hindsight, it was clear that I wanted out.

~

It was a cold Monday night in January 2019 when Ash and I decided to move to Melbourne. He had an Australian passport, so the possibility had played in our minds since we visited the country a year earlier. I told my manager two days later.

London was a depressing place to be. The expense, the dreariness, the hisses of Brexit Brexit Brexit everywhere. I was desperate to be free of my parents' endless dysfunction. Tilly would have to move to the Peak District with Ash's mum, but they got on well. I trusted her.

I went back to Cardiff to tell my family in person. I felt I owed them that. I had already told Bee, who I felt I was abandoning again. My dad drove me to Barry to visit Nan and Grandad. I hadn't said anything to my parents yet. We let ourselves in, hugged, kicked off our shoes. I sat on the fuzzy beige carpet with my back against the radiator. Grandad was next to me in his armchair. He and Uncle Steve discussed last week's skittles while my dad read the paper.

Grandad was frail by then, but he spoke more that day than ever. It was almost like he knew he might not get another chance. This man of few words began telling me stories from the 1940s. Tales of fruit for Christmas, their Anderson shelter out back. He didn't have long left. None of us would have guessed that his son would follow so soon.

As my dad and I drove home through Wenvoe, I blurted out, 'I have something to tell you.'

He froze. I added in a single breath, 'I'm moving to Melbourne.'

He relaxed and slapped the steering wheel. 'That's fantastic.'

A quarter of an hour later, we were passing through Fairwater when flashes of blue blazoned in the rearview mirror. Cars drew apart, but my dad slowed and stayed in the middle of the road.

I turned to look over my shoulder. 'Police coming, Dad, you'd better pull over.'

'Fuck 'em,' he said. 'Bunch of gangsters.'

The van nudged up behind us, searching for a gap.

'Dad, seriously, it could be a crash.'

'Hope *they* fucking crash, good riddance.' He stared ahead, ignoring the siren.

'Move, Dad! Please!'

He ragged leftwards, the van sped past, and I resurrected a light tone. I was heading back to London the next day and grateful he was sober, if not particularly nice. I told my mum the news that afternoon. She said it was her 'worst nightmare' and refused to speak to me about it.

In the morning, just before I left, my dad and I were sat together in the conservatory of Coffee #1, the Wellfield Road branch. We looked at a map of the world on my phone.

'We could meet midway in India, you know, while I'm out there in Australia,' I suggested, heartened that he was supporting me. 'We've always wanted to go there, haven't we, Kerala, can you imagine?'

He nodded. '100 per cent. Let's make it happen.'

~

The next month, my dad came to London by train. He had a work thing, he said, and wanted to have lunch with me at the National Liberal Club. Wednesday 13 February 2019. It was a grey, heavy day.

On my way to work that morning, I detoured to Waterstones Piccadilly. Too early, the doors were still locked. I waited in the drizzle and checked which floor I'd need. Lower Ground. The store opened. I hurried down past the display of globes and stacked luggage. Travel, there it was. *Lonely Planet: India*. I wrote a card about life in technicolour and tucked it between the pages for him.

I darted out a little early for my lunch-break so I could get over to Embankment in time. I arrived before my dad and hovered in the arched doorway. We were supposed to meet at noon. I waited twenty minutes, pacing the carpet, treading it thinner and thinner. The grandeur of my dad's dreams was fading, his horizons shrinking. Even before he arrived, I knew he wouldn't be him. Years of training meant I could sense it. I'd soon be face to face with the nightmare I was trying, by day, to escape.

It was another ten minutes before he fell from a taxi, noosing his polka dot tie. I followed him feebly through the glassy doors. We didn't go straight to our table. Instead, we stood on the terrace overlooking the Thames. I pointed out, matter of fact, that he was extremely drunk. He didn't have much to say about it. Nor did I. I gave him the book and card. I looked at his face against the cityscape. There was something newly vulnerable about him. I felt an engulfing wave of grief.

In theory, like always, I had to make a call: stay or go. It didn't feel like that at the time. I was programmed not to let my dad down, not to hurt his feelings. He had looked forward to this lunch, drunk or not. He had been keen to visit this club. I couldn't walk out of here and disappoint him. I couldn't leave.

We were seated. To the staff, I must have appeared calm, resigned. I smiled and chatted lightly. I pointedly called him 'Dad' in front of the waiters, like I always did. I was twenty-five, he was fifty-three. Sometimes the relatively narrow age gap could be an awkward point of error. 'What are you having, Dad?' I'd never get to say that again. 'Dad.'

He ordered oysters, of all things. Sloshing, bloodshot, he toppled my world down his throat. Six times, to be precise. A final briny flourish. His glazed eyes slipped past me. He spluttered self-righteously. He told me, proudly, that he had called out the other lawyers at the work event for being sexist about the waitresses.

'Believe me, I won't get invited back,' he said, awaiting my applause.

I had to go. I needed to rush for a meeting. I hurried to the toilets on my way out and bumped into my dad as I left. I was on the stairs above him, looking down. I remember his expression. Crinkled eyes, sloppily happy. It was the last time I ever saw my dad.

Sprinting along Embankment afterwards, lunch-break long overrun, I reassembled the unfazeable face I was so practised at wearing. Behind it I felt utterly drained by the exertion of feigning belief that he'd get better. He had been sober for a little while this time. Another tense, tiring, dispiriting while. I was quite heartbroken that day.

I slipped back into my open, familial workspace in Fitzrovia. A teammate asked how my lunch was and I nodded amiably. After our meeting I watered my windowsill fittonia, made a cup of tea, then sat to breathe slowly in front of my screen, keyboard, mouse. The tasks weren't trivial here. I was good at my job, and I adored my colleagues. We supported freelance journalists in crisis. I could make a difference here. That was different.

My mum texted a few days later, asking why my dad and I had ordered a bottle of fancy wine at lunch. She had found a receipt in his jacket. I sent a short, sharp reply saying it obviously must have been after I left. And then I went totally silent, even when he re-emerged from his binge after a month:

Visit to Cardiff?

Tue 12 Mar 2019 12:16 PM

When I met you in London you mentioned that you would be in Cardiff between 13–15 March. Are you still planning to come home tomorrow? It would be fantastic to see you. Your mum is very down at the moment – she is really upset that you are not communicating with her. Me and Danny are also extremely sad about it all. Let me know.
Love
Dad

I didn't respond. I was gone, phone dangling by the cord. I had a feeling it might be for good. Being his daughter, I now understood, meant being bleary to everyone else, even myself. I had to vanish. It was simpler, at the time, to forget how he had emailed the restaurant to check options for me before we met:

FW: NLC – Dining Room booking

Mon 11 Feb 2019 12:55 PM

I wish to book a table at your club for Wednesday lunchtime for me and my daughter, Sophie (who lives and works in London).
What is the earliest we could book a table for? I know that she is hoping to be back at work (which is very near to the Club) by 2.00pm or thereabouts.
Sophie does not eat meat so it would be good if we could view your menu for Wednesday if that is possible.
Many thanks
Mike

For him and his daughter, Sophie, who he would never see again.

On the Friday after my dad's email about coming home, Ash and I hired a van to take Tilly north. We stuffed the back with things we couldn't bring with us to Australia. Tilly sat between us on the front seat. She howled and vomited before we had even got out of London. She wasn't a good traveller.

When we arrived, Tilly glanced at her new home then snuggled into Ash's mum's lap. She was very adaptable. A family trait. The next day, she spotted cows from the window and couldn't take her eyes off these strange countryside creatures. We laughed.

On Sunday morning, Tilly pawed her way under our duvet and tucked under my arm like she had done since I was eleven. I pulled the blankets over my head and sobbed into her old-lady fur. I sensed I wouldn't see her again either. It felt like another goodbye I couldn't explain to a loved one, even if it were for the best.

II
2019–2022

a displaced refugee

And yet if it weren't for Australia, I might have imploded. I needed the change of scene, the distance, the sunshine. We left London for Melbourne on 1 April 2019, just as the UK was preparing to leave the EU.

For our first fortnight, Ash and I hired a camper van and explored the tropical north's national parks. Meanwhile, back in Cardiff, armed police had to break into my family's house. My dad was insisting on living there. I think my mum and siblings were squashed in together at the dead-end terrace.

Inside the house, the police found a lot of blood and a cryptic note about 'my son'. I woke to photos of all this from my mum. She didn't want me to miss out, I suppose. The crimson looked even more wrong now, at odds with the deep blue skies above me.

I emailed the police from the back of our camper van. It was the first time I had done anything like this, but I was so far away and needed to feel less helpless:

Re: Urgent concern for family's safety

Sun 14 Apr 2019 4:02 AM

Hello,

My name is Sophie and I'm the elder daughter of [redacted], who has been arrested numerous times by South Wales Police and will be on your records.

This is a confidential email to raise serious concerns about the safety of my mother, brother, and sister in light of my father's extremely unstable mental state. I now live abroad and have been generally estranged from my father for several years, but I receive partial/sporadic updates from my immediate family about the highly volatile situation they are facing in Cardiff. I am increasingly anxious that my father may need to be sectioned under the Mental Health Act else he is likely to do harm to himself and/or others.

Please do get back to me as soon as possible; I am keen to learn of any measures that SWP are taking to monitor my father and ensure that my family members are as safe as possible.

Many thanks,
Sophie

It didn't achieve anything. After that I tried to relax, to let go. We rented a bungalow in a dreamy, lilac neighbourhood in Naarm, Melbourne, all jacaranda trees and velvet flat whites. It felt like home from the get-go. Surely 10,622 miles was enough to feel safer, at least by day, when I had my eyes open.

I still woke drenched in sweat. He was only two flights away, and right there in my nightmares. I avoided sharing where I lived or worked on social media. It's absurd in hindsight, but I looked both ways before leaving my office, at a women's rights agency, just in case. I defended my space as if my life depended on it. There was a constant rumble of worry in my stomach, a gnawing hunger for peace and sanctuary.

One afternoon, a colleague asked if I had read Sally Rooney's *Conversations with Friends*. I said I was a fan. She suggested we start a book club with some of the other women at the agency. We began meeting at each other's homes to chat and laugh. They were fiery and hilarious, kind and intelligent. That conversation found me my first friends in Australia.

~

Over time, life became lighter, skies higher. Ash and I cycled to work each day. Our faces caught the sun, warm even in winter, as we whooshed up and down Melbourne's hills. I got back into running. In the evenings, I bounded along beside the winding, eucalypt-lined creek that borrows its name from the Wurundjeri-willam language: Merri Merri, very rocky. A misnomer: this place soothed and smoothed my forehead's creases.

In the trees, kookaburras chuckled and Australian magpies warbled their joyful songs. Late into our first year there, spring span the banks of wattle golden. I was twenty-six by then, and I felt vigorous and youthful in a way that was new to me.

Ash and I spent more and more time outdoors. We met friends for walks in the Dandenong Ranges, misty temperate rainforest rolling with fern gullies and steep ash trees, less than an hour away. We larked about in the sea, leaping and shrieking as the waves peaked. We met up to paint together in Edinburgh Gardens, lazing in the languid heat.

Ash's family came over for Christmas. We had a barbecue in our backyard, sweltering in the 30°C heat, then went to New Zealand to greet the new year. I saw the beauty in the pearly glaciers, the purple lupin fields, the green mussels. We hiked and ran, drank and swam in gaspingly cold water. We sipped cans of Garage Project on Lake Wānaka's shore. I read a novel by Elsa Morante and listened to Courtney Barnett.

We set up camp by Lake Te Anau on New Year's Eve and stuck a bottle of sparkling wine into the sand, hoping the tide would cool it. A middle-aged group took pity and gave us a spot in their esky. I wrote *2020* in hopeful shells.

On New Year's Day, we woke early to a strange smell and an eerie tinge to the world. Smoke, with a sepia filter.

'They must be burning something in town,' I shrugged.

We made our coffee and porridge. I shivered. There was a chill in the air. We folded up our tent and walked quickly back to our car. Thick clouds hung low. It was only later that we realised the smoke had carried over from the Australian bushfires. They had been raging for weeks.

We went to our next stop, Milford Sound, and kayaked below bellowing waterfalls. Negative ions, everywhere. We soaked them up, then headed off for our three-day hike on Mount Aspiring. On our ascent to a small red hut, it felt like we were the only people for miles around. We crossed rickety bridges and clambered up tree roots, passing no one else.

When we reached the peak, we saw the bushfire smoke had dyed the snow brown. We tried to drink from the water barrel and spat it out when the carbon hit our taste buds.

'It's like lapsang souchong,' Ash said. We drowned it out as much as we could with peppermint teabags.

That night I crept out of bed to go to the outdoor toilet. I stepped outside into a sky that was so clear and pure and starlit that I gasped. Its depth and vastness overwhelmed me. I scampered, head down and scared of all those worlds beyond ours.

The following day I was heavy with regret, wishing I had woken Ash to come and see. I went out again in the early hours, ready, hyped, but the clouds hid it all and kept life small. We left the next morning in the pouring rain. I promised myself I wouldn't look away if I ever met that sky again.

Back in Melbourne, the burning apocalypse went on and on. The city was ominously orange around the clock. That summer, the fires killed or displaced three billion animals. To avoid inhaling all the smoke, people wore masks. A precursor of what was to come. One lunch-break I watched in disbelief as a woman lifted her mask to take a drag from a cigarette.

~

After the smoke had cleared, Bee flew over to stay with us for two weeks. I was beside myself with excitement. I drove to the airport to fetch her and stood holding a handmade sign with her name. I took the fortnight off from work and showed her all my favourite places. We went to wildlife sanctuaries, vineyards, beaches, galleries. We made tuna pasta and stopped to stroke every cat we encountered.

Ash joined us for a weekend road trip to Phillip Island. We watched little penguins waddle in from the sea at dusk and followed gigantic rays sashaying by a pier. We took a selfie with a can printed *Share a Coke with Sis*. We ate flake and chips, and scanned the sand for pretty shells. We went for Korean food and stayed out late. G&Ts for Bee, beers for Ash and me. We strolled back to our B&B, arms linked, laughing at everything and living in the moment, doing our best to forget home.

On the Sunday I woke to WhatsApps from Lisa saying not to worry. *Your dad has been found*, she wrote. We hadn't even known he was missing again, but apparently the police appeal had been on everyone's Facebook feeds. He was pretty much homeless by then. He had been living on and off with Nan in Barry, but she couldn't do it anymore. He was leaving her front door wide open at night when he went out into the dark. Her nerves were frayed. He was hurting her, even if he didn't mean to. The neighbours were concerned. I looked up the post while Bee showered.

South Wales Police
Bridgend and Vale of Glamorgan
27 mins

Can you help us?

We are appealing for information concerning the whereabouts of [redacted] who has been reported as missing ... See more

He was unshaven in the photo, nearly bearded. His hair was greying at the sides. His mouth wasn't quite smiling, but there was a hint of light in his eyes. The spitting image of mine, those eyes, heavy-lidded and thin. The sun lit the right side of his face. I knew instinctively he was by the sea too. I peered at my screen and, yes, there was sand behind him.

It was a reminder not to get too relaxed. Bee didn't want to talk about the family situation. We were on holiday mode, after all.

On our last night together we went to a gig at Melbourne Zoo. We sat on a picnic blanket at sunset, swaying to Weyes Blood and Julia Jacklin. We were on a mad one, necking wine and trying not to count down the hours until her flight.

As we walked back I was distracted, chatting with Ash, and Bee somehow vanished just a minute or so away from our home. I started panicking, tearfully calling her name as I wandered around my street. I rang and texted but got no reply. Ash told me to chill out. She's a grown-up, he said, just leave the door unlocked. Bee came back a while later. Turned out she had been invited into a house party a few doors up, but the boys there were weird. The next day we had a hungover brunch then I dropped her at the airport. On my drive home I missed her already. She was my whole family.

~

Bee was our last visitor to Australia. Two weeks later, on Sunday 15 March, we hosted a barbecue for friends. Asparagus, corn on the cob, plant-based burgers, the works. The next day we were told to fetch our laptops then stay at home for the foreseeable future. I never went back to the office and, I'll be honest, I preferred remote work. The freedom brought out the best in me.

Each morning before we sat at our desks, Ash and I went for a walk with flasks of coffee. That autumn gave us clear skies and sunshine. We watched the rainbow lorikeets flit among the leaves, avoiding eye contact with the soldiers and police who patrolled our park. Sellotaped to a nearby lamp post was a hand-written note by a child called Ziggy. He listed the steps required to stay safe from the coronavirus. *I think you can do it*, Ziggy wrote at the end.

People hung up signs and flags, like STAY STRONG. I ♥ U. Our next-door neighbour worked at the local cat shelter and arranged for us to start fostering cats, given we'd be home for a while. I went to fetch the first one in late March. Her name was Lara Jane and she was an absolute diva.

I did a video call with my oldest friends, Lisa and Pip. Mates since we were four. We waved at each other and took screenshots. It was all still a novelty.

It was at this time that my mum decided to divorce my dad, for real. He had been fired from his job and had no fixed address. He stayed with Nan until she could no longer endure it. Drifting between tents and homeless shelters, he still had a lawyer. My mum refused to get legal help, citing money worries, and instead relied on me and her brother. I drafted statements to support her in the hearings, dying inside from the reliving of it all.

The panic and fear rose up again, like a wave, stinging my eyes and choking my throat. I had to walk away from a work video call in our bedroom, a lockdown check-in on how we were all doing. Ash crept in to shut the screen while I wiped my eyes in our bathroom. Everything was blurring again, but this time I leapt away just before it submerged me.

Books helped my mind settle. I was reading my way around the world via women writers. I had set off in June 2018, and two years on I was nearing the end of my journey. I noted lines that resonated, such as: *I read as if books could loosen the noose tightening around my throat* from Mauritian author Ananda Devi's novella *Eve Out of her Ruins*, translated by Jeffrey Zuckerman. I found things in common with writers from every continent. I learned about the resilience of women far away and nearby, about violence and defiance, about empowerment and solidarity, about the beauty that can be seen even in lives more difficult than mine.

I did regular video calls with friends from back home. We ate toast slathered with baked beans and cheese, their breakfast, my tea. I joined my friend Maysa's virtual belly-dancing class.

Two months into the pandemic, I started working with the Victorian Government. 'Staying apart keeps us together,' we told the public. My colleagues were lovely. I had always been so lucky like that. I sat on the patio for our cheery morning calls, the winter sun stroking my cheeks. I spoke with diverse communities about what they wanted from the Minister, then weaved their wishes into her briefings and speeches. I enjoyed the work we did.

Just before daybreak on Fridays, I fumbled for my running kit in the dark and went for a run with a friend in Princes Park. We did a few laps while the sun rose, then got takeaway coffee from Wide Open Road's hole in the wall. We sipped oat flat whites, dawdling to chat. It was the only socialising that we were permitted. One morning I told her a bit about my family. She was open-mouthed.

As usual, my mum was forwarding everything that my dad sent her. I asked her to stop, but it was a force of habit. She had done it since I was a kid. His messages made me feel sick. He still went running as well:

Re: Settlement

Wed 23 Sep 2020 7:57 AM

I am very depressed, stressed and agitated. I don't sleep properly, even if I go running for hours at the end of the day. I can't concentrate at the moment. You had me evicted from our home when I was very ill. I thought that the 'deal' when we got married was that it was forever 'in sickness or in health'?
Our home was 'the needle in my compass'. I belong with you – and at our home. Virtually everything I enjoyed doing – and was good at doing – happened in or close to our home. If I ever get any sleep in the places I am these days, when I wake up I still think/hope that I am waking up in our bed. I also enjoyed looking at the mutts

*sleeping very contentedly in front of our roaring fire in the winter.
I am a displaced refugee in situations that make no sense to me.
Then you divorced me, which broke my heart ...*

A displaced refugee. His distortions, or delusions, still managed to shock me.

He was waging a battle against what he now knew was long going, *hirmynd*, by his own doing. Our beautiful life all together, disintegrating right in front of him. Only, he realised this too late.

Eventually, I got an email from the Court that ended all the horrific back-and-forth. They said I would have to join a video call with my dad as cross-examiner. The sky sank. The dense air gagged me. I sent a single line of defeat, quitting the game and fleeing again. By now it was spring in the southern hemisphere, and Melbourne was radiant. I focused my attention on things that brought me joy: reading, writing, running. Good sapped bad, like it always had for me. *My name is Sophie ... I love my world.*

Restrictions temporarily eased around the time of our second Christmas out there. Ash and I went to Byron Bay and stayed first in a rainforest eco-home, then in a bell tent. On Christmas Eve, a small creature tried to pinch the Ferrero Rochers left out by our host. We found the nibbled loot by a hole gnawed into the canvas. Merry Christmas! We laughed. I went for a run under a crystal sky and tried to forget the screenshot I had woken up to from my mum. A WalesOnline article. No one I knew from journalism school in the byline, thankfully.

The homeless people who had a proper Christmas dinner thanks to the people who gave up theirs

A warm meal and a warm welcome has been offered by volunteers across Wales

There was a photo midway down. A man rested his right hand on a girl's back. Hood up, her age was hard to judge, but she looked like a child. He was grinning, facing her way, while she stared into the lens, eyes blank. The caption: *People enjoying meals in their bubbles at The Huggard.*

Their bubbles, his bubble. My dad. I might not have guessed if not for his khaki jacket. Between them, my dad and the blank-eyed girl, were two uncracked crackers, one white, one red with polka dots. His pop fizzed, half drunk, in a see-through plastic cup. He had guzzled most of his dinner. Her meal lay untouched.

I shook it away as Ash and I prepared our avocado on toast. I made us two glasses of Buck's Fizz and took pictures in my floaty dress. We went for a four-course plant-based lunch al fresco at a bougie restaurant. I ran into the sea and leapt around in the buffeting surf while Ash read his book. I was happy and sad and all the things in between.

god I was mental

As far as pandemic set-ups go, Ash and I were as lucky as it gets. We were healthy and fit. We had our own space. We had secure jobs that could be done from the safety of home.

Even so, the extremity of it all got into our heads. Life in Melbourne was increasingly frazzled. The rollercoaster rules and curfews, the unpredictability of snap lockdowns, the hard border half a world away from our family and friends.

After months of agonising, we decided to return to the UK. We hadn't gone to Australia with an end-date in mind, but we couldn't stay without any sense of when we might next see everyone we loved. It was not straightforward to get out. As an Australian citizen, Ash had to complete paperwork. Flights were hard to come by, with many cancelled even if scheduled.

In spring 2021 we managed to get on a flight home. All the shutters were down in the international departures lounge. There was no one around. The jumbo jet had a total of seven passengers including us. I asked if there was any room in first class, only half joking. The airline staff didn't laugh.

We landed home a day later. I beelined to M&S for an egg and watercress sandwich. We unpacked our two suitcases in a beautiful corner of the southwest Peak District, near Ash's family, until we found a home of our own.

A day or two in, it snowed. Our tans looked out of sync with our surroundings. Hills seasoned with sheep. Daffodils, bluebells. Restrictions were easing. I was able to surprise Bee for her birthday, conspiring with her partner, Lloyd, to gatecrash their trip to Machynlleth. We settled into two shepherd huts overlooking the sea. The sunset swirled around the sky the evening we arrived. We went for brisk walks on the beach and rambled across the hillsides in the drizzle. It was *perffaith*, perfect.

~

I went to Cardiff just once between my homecoming and my dad's death that December. I mostly avoided my hometown while he was stumbling around it. The trip was uneventful, fun even, despite the fact that I was on edge at the possibility of bumping into him. My siblings and I went to the coast at Ogmore and danced by the waves. Danny made us laugh.

After a few days, I was due to head back up north to the Peak District. Bee gave me a lift to Cardiff Central. She mentioned that our dad had left some notes in her car when she bumped into him recently, jottings from his time in prison and on the streets. He had been sentenced to a month in HMP Cardiff for breaking a non-molestation order preventing him from going to Nan's.

Bee clicked open the glovebox and the notes tipped onto my lap. I took photos on my phone so I could read them once home. Bee pulled into the back car park, where police were taping off a crime scene. We looked at the vans and ambulance. The hostel where our dad had been placed was only a few minutes away. He was where our minds darted at signs of emergencies.

'When did you last see him?' I asked quickly.

'Last week,' she said. 'I drove past him. Took him to A&E. They said he was alright, somehow.'

'That man is a machine,' I replied.

Bee spotted our dad a lot while out and about. Cardiff is a small world, but sometimes she went looking for him just to know he was still alive. He slept rough for much of the pandemic, looking less and less recognisable. I occasionally saw photos from Bee or our mum. His thick dark hair had grown shaggy, his face red, his clothes dirty. He was thin, a little hunched. He had been suffering with symptoms of long covid and was usually bruised and battered, so she drove him to the Heath to get checked out. The Heath, where he saw us coming into the world and she saw him slowly going from it.

We said bye, distracted. I heaved my rucksack from the boot and headed to the barriers, opening Twitter as I walked. I typed into the search bar: *Cardiff train station police*. Nothing. *Accident Cardiff train.* Nothing. *Cardiff homeless station.* Still nothing. I scanned WalesOnline, then the Google News tab. Nothing. I was becoming anxious, then Bee texted:

I just drove past dad walking down the road by Splott

> *Kidding? Wtf are the chances*
> *Did he look normal?*

I actually pulled over and had a weirdly alright conversation with him
I usually wouldn't have, but I think I was a little bit relieved because of what we'd just seen

> *What was he saying?*

He just asked about everyone and it was quite civil

Was he sober?

Yeah

I was showing him the letters that he'd left in my car a few months ago and he was laughing and saying, 'god I was mental'
I showed him this picture of us three

Did he like the pic?

Yeah, did ask why Danny is so fat though

She sent a second photo, taken just then, of our dad reading his notes in her passenger seat. A mirror image of me from ten minutes before. It had been over two years since I had seen him on that grey lunch-break in London. Today he looked completely himself. Smiling, bronzed, hair neatly shorn. Reading glasses on. In his Marine Nationale top, a favourite, its logo an anchor interlaced with sailing rope. The car door is left open in the photo. Our dad never stayed for long. I couldn't tell if I felt glad about this near-miss, or upset, or fearful, so I stared out of the train window and listened to my playlist of his favourite songs.

It's a lifestyle, trying to predict the unthinkable. We were always ready for it.

~

Australia's bushfires had pushed me to look for an environmental job. In June, I joined a small team working on a climate podcast. For the first time ever, I found my working hours unsettling. Calls with my manager left me feeling belittled, disoriented. Out of kilter. Each evening I shut my laptop and ran up into the peaks to regain my footing.

I thought about my dad a lot while I ran, and one night I impulsively wrote a message to him. I was undecided on whether it was a good idea to send it. Did I want to be in contact? Would I regret never reaching out? I slept on it, then clicked send during my lunch-break the next day:

Seeing the beauty

Wed 4 Aug 2021 12:43 PM

Hello Dad,

It's been over two years, but every day I keep in mind all that you taught me. I paused on yesterday's run to take in the sunset rays behind the wildflowers. Here's what I saw.

It's exciting to be back on this side of the world. I visited Wales in June and Danny entertained me with a jig. The sea was sparkling and we soaked up the negative ions. In Australia, Ash and I began going on big long walks each weekend and realised we're happiest when surrounded by nature, so we want to live in the countryside from now on. I think it's the answer. (What's the question?)

I hope you're finding ways to be well and see the beauty too.

Love,
Soph – elder daughter

I emailed it to him, unsure if he'd get it. A while later I told Bee, who said he didn't have any way to access his inbox. I emailed it to her and she gave him a printout when they next crossed paths. He read it on a bench by the sea in Penarth, she said, as well as a short story I had written about him. Bee had printed that too. My story ended with the word *brink*. I left his future up to him. She said he laughed at parts and remarked, 'All sounds about right.'

~

A few months back I had learned about Hebden Bridge, a town in West Yorkshire, through a publisher I followed on Twitter. Their tweets of canals and old mills always made me feel peaceful. We had nowhere in particular to be, so I suggested a visit. Within just a few hours of pottering around the cobbles and crafty bars and quiet woodlands we knew the valley would become our next home.

In November, Ash and I moved to an old stone cottage ten minutes uphill from Hebden.

The beech woods around us were aflame that autumn. We unpacked our things, then I took a train to Glasgow for COP26. The city was a surreal stage of panels, protests, police, pantomime. There were hordes of conference-goers everywhere, claiming to be the authority on how we might best divert the apocalypse. I kept myself busy, making notes on ways to save the world.

On the last night, we went dancing in the face of crisis. Drunk and tired, I shovelled down hot chips at an ungodly hour in a doorway. A homeless man apologised for bothering me but could I spare some change? I was uninhibited, excitable. I don't know how I replied, but we started chatting. He sat down beside me. Talk turned to the pandemic, as it always did then.

'Me, I'm not getting the jab,' he said.

I exploded into lecture mode, reeling about responsibilities.

He turned his palms to the grey night sky. 'Why would *I* trust the authorities?'

I pushed on, impatient, eager to change his mind. 'If not for you, think of others.'

He resisted, both of us unlistening until emotion reached my eyes.

'You should know,' I raised my voice, 'that my dad is homeless and I'm told he has long covid.'

The man's face stilled, believing me instantly despite the silly lanyard around my neck.

'I doubt he got the vaccine,' I was spilling over with tears now, chips set aside, 'but I wish he had.'

The man shook his head, sincere as anything, shoulders hunched with sorrow.

'I'm so sorry about your dad. I'm so sorry,' he said.

He said it over and over while I let tears leak down my face, as if I was the victim in all this. A colleague tugged me away, confused by my outburst. We queued to re-enter the salsa bar. The man passed by the line of people. We caught eyes once more, and he called across with a solemnity I've never forgotten.

'I really am sorry about your dad.'

I nodded. He went on his way. If I did ask his name, I don't recall it. I took a train home the next day, then promptly tested positive for covid. COP was a superspreader, I suspect.

~

Bee sometimes shared bits of what our dad's existence had become by then. Just fragments, piecemeal. She mostly didn't want to talk about it.

One fragment: our dad convulsing in her car, a seizure induced by a sudden, self-imposed attempt at sobriety. Bee had to pull over outside Penylan Fish Bar while he shuddered in the passenger seat. Our neighbour Karim was no longer behind the counter. He had died of covid. His son was just two months older than me, too young to lose a parent.

Another fragment: our dad disappearing ahead of an important meeting. Bee went looking for him the day before, driving around near the hostel where he had been allotted a room. She found him and took him to a hotel, hoping he'd take the chance for a bit of peace and quiet. She told our dad to scrub up, eat something nice, and stay where she could find him. Early the next day, she went to fetch him for the meeting. The door was ajar. The bed was empty. She hurried to her car to start looking again. She was circling the Magic Roundabout when he stumbled out in front of her.

'Soph, I'm not kidding, I literally almost drove right into him,' she said, 'Can you imagine?'

I couldn't.

Even so, Bee's texts struck a hopeful note in the last week of November:

I don't know if this is even relevant
But Dad has a phone now, I bumped into him the other day – he's trying to sort himself out

> *Was he drunk or sober?*

He has a drink every day, because you can't just stop drinking unless you have professional help 24 seven

> *Yep*

But he was completely with it
Best I've seen him in a while
He looked good as well, haircut and everything

I saved the number into my phone: *Dad – Nov 2021*. I didn't think I'd do anything with it, at least not immediately. I'd wait and see. For years I had wondered when the inevitable would happen, but momentarily I wondered if—

khaki is Persian for dust

27 December 2021. It's an hour since Lisa told me he's gone, my dad. My dad has died. It has happened, the loss I had anticipated for so long.

I lie flat on the living room rug and let our kittens pitter-patter over me. I cry silently for a minute or so, until I realise it's confusing the cats and discomfiting Ash, who has made me a cup of tea. I sip and remember with a shudder that I drank an IPA called Life & Death with my friends over lunch. Little did I know, while I enjoyed my beer, that my dad had already been found dead.

I go upstairs and sit in bed to call Bee. I hold my voice tight, controlled, trying to perform my role as elder sister. I say comforting things. It is the least I can do. I'm twenty-eight, she's twenty-two. It was her door that the police knocked. She had been painting a wall in her living room.

Bee was by far the closest and kindest to our dad over this last year or so, all those hours spent driving to find him, feed him, get him checked over at the Heath. Such a cornerstone. That hospital he brought each of us home from, where he taught us how to stay afloat and swim. I reassure her about the peace he has found now.

'I'm convinced of it,' I say, while she hyperventilates.

Next I ring my mum. She is hysterical.

'How do I go on?' she cries, 'You can't keep pushing us away.'

I hold my phone at a distance, wrist tense with the strain. I ask if Danny's there. He is. I swallow and lightly ask him what he's up to.

'Wondering where my dinner's got to,' he says.

Danny lists those he expects our dad's death will upset. From shock or autism, he omits himself. Inseparable across Danny's childhood, they weren't allowed to see each other in recent years.

'Have a good evening, Soph.' He hangs up.

One more call for me to make, for now. To Nan, whose voice is hoarse and full of love.

'I always left the key where I knew he could find it,' she says. 'Please, Soph, tell me something happy from your life.'

I hear him here in this last line.

In the end, I suppose, it might have been a kind of happiness, though reckless and othered and wild, tumbling from gutter to gutter, and fighting, grinning, drinking, drinking, drinking until his load lightened and the chaos spiralled. At times I despised him in the dusk of his life. The things he did, said, wrote. Now, I guess, I might finally miss the dawns with the dad who raised me.

∼

I have to go back, obviously. In the morning I head to the train station. The Hebden Bridge ticket officer winces at the triple-figured price of my journey to Cardiff.

'Gotta plan in advance,' he advises.

I laugh. 'Serves me right, hey, for travelling last-minute.'

I change at Leeds and scan for a seat as I board. Relief unclenches my shoulders as I spot a space next to a woman, my preferred option. I wedge my bag between my ankles and take out a notepad. As if on cue, the woman begins coughing her lungs up. I regret sitting here within a minute, but am too British to back out.

She's mid-fifties, I'd guess. Same age as my parents. My parent. I tighten my mask's cords behind my ears and pray I won't give Nan the virus. How do you keep your distance when the person between you has just died? The woman chugs water from a plastic bottle. We catch eyes. I ease my face into a smile. Her floodgates open.

'I'm not well, love,' she croaks. 'I'll go down the hospital when I'm back. Spent Christmas at my daughter's but couldn't hack my thieving son-in-law.'

She goes on. Half an hour, an hour, I lose track. In a nutshell: 'an addict, I am, love, been in 'n out of custody. Was always gonna get me, 'cos drink killed me dad, like. And now I'm gonna be evicted from me flat and all. It's no life, no life.'

Words course from her while I murmur pathetic notes of comfort, like how great it is that she's drinking lots of water. I don't mention why I'm travelling. The festive season doesn't have room for too many stories like ours.

The woman asks what I'll be writing. I look at the biro and empty notepad in my lap, as much a mystery to me at this stage.

'A book,' I reply. 'About life and stuff.'

'Wow.' She nudges me. 'Good for you, eh!'

Thing is, I know there'll be nothing written if I stay, with over two hours until my next change. I've always had an impulse to record all this as it happens, to keep it clear in my mind. I guess it's a defence mechanism, a need for self-control. An anchoring.

'I'm off to get a tea,' I say, 'then I need to find a forward-facing seat. Feeling a bit queasy.'

True, if skewed excuses. 'It was nice to meet you,' I add.

She pats my arm. Her hand is chilly and her expression is warm. I feel so guilty for leaving her alone. I stand and walk away, for my own sake, the way I did from him.

'Good luck with your writing,' she wheezes, 'and hey, maybe I'll be in your book someday.'

Two carriages down, I sip tea in my own pair of seats. A luxury I don't deserve, all this space here, all this gaping time. I text Ash, describing the woman to him, repeating things she told me.

I swear the UK is in a really bad way, I write.

Would she still be alive, I wonder, if these lines ever do make it to print?

~

I arrive at Cardiff Central at 6:21 pm. The sky has the haze of the urban. The disused brewery tower's white letters taunt me, lurking above the platform's green serrated roof.

BRAINS

Brains was my dad's main client back in the day. A constant feature of my childhood. He bragged about his big-deal deals, all the functions he'd come home from frothing and dysfunctional. For years my mind has filtered for these episodes, holding fast to reasons for keeping him at a distance. Now I suppose it's safe to reset. I can remember all the other things, how fun and funny and supportive he was, all the excuses we made for his one big flaw.

Bee's partner, Lloyd pulls into Cardiff Central's car park. Bee is in the passenger seat. I put her in the back with me and hold her close. She's sobbing, shaking. I don't cry, though I could. We go to hers. Their dogs nuzzle us on the sofa. My friend Milno comes over and we order food. The TV is on, muted with subtitles. No one is watching it. I'm not sure what we talk about. Nonsense, I imagine.

Our mum lets herself in and sits on a chair in the corner. Within ten minutes, she has left in floods of tears. Bee doesn't eat a thing. Me, I'm ravenous, devouring a whole box of noodles. Bee has no spare bed and the dogs sleep on the sofa, so I go to stay at Milno's. When we get in, her partner is hosting friends. I make small talk then head upstairs.

Early the next day, I quietly pull on my trainers and run back over to Bee's. I knock, but succeed only in waking the dogs. I probably should have texted. Once she's up, we take the dogs to Roath's flower gardens down the road. While we walk, Bee's phone rings with an unknown number. She stares in horror. I pick up the call. It's the

Coroner's Service. I tell them to switch me in for next of kin. I have to step up now after my years-long withdrawal.

We get breakfast at Juno Lounge, Wellfield Road. It's a place I've been many times, including for one or two ill-fated dates a decade ago. While we wait to be seated I take a local massage leaflet, blank on the back, from the front table. I have to set out options for what we'll do about the body. Our dad's. I'm not using my journal for that. We're pointed towards a space at the back. We order eggs Florentine, then I use my clearest, unjoined handwriting to bullet-point ways we could lay our dad to rest. He hated graveyards.

'Remember how he loved pointing out all the "dead space" each time we passed Cathays Cemetery,' I say to Bee. 'We need somewhere, like, ungloomy for him.'

I list Cardiff and The Vale Natural Burial Meadow as an option. Milno had told me about it. Trees, birds, estuary views. It would suit him. Somewhere for the wanderer to put down roots. Or, I muse aloud, we could do a cremation and scattering by the sea?

Hm. I imagine the face my mum would pull if I even utter the word 'cremation'. She arrives, het up, multiple dogs in tow. Bee and I try to keep it low-key, which I realise might translate frostily given the circumstances. My mum chooses drama and asks why I hate her.

'I don't,' I say, folding the leaflet and tapping my biro. 'We'll go with the meadow,' I decide.

~

Bee and I drive to Barry after breakfast. We let ourselves in, hug Nan, kick off our shoes. Nan fills floral cups and saucers with PG Tips then plates up chocolate digestives. Her hands tremble. She looks far older than when I left for Australia. Her hair has gone from dark purply-brown to stark white. She hovers on the kitchen tiles, clutching a used tissue. Her eyes are silently streaming.

'I told you, didn't I, Soph, I always left the key where I knew he could find it if— if he wanted.'

Uncle Steve comes over. He talks nonstop. About all sorts, I don't remember quite what. There was a long anecdote about his mates down the caravan park. It's nice, normal. There's barely a mention of our dad, his brother. It's hard to know what to say about that.

I go to the upstairs bathroom, then walk along the landing to the room where my dad had slept. Or not slept, more accurately. The bed is covered in books, now under dust sheets. He must have left them here before the restraining order.

It's only now that my mind is quieter, that I can see him more clearly, that I sense he never set out to hurt us. He just hurt us by accident. It's only with hindsight that it seems far-fetched to have thought he might try to kill us. At times, while he was alive but unrecognisable, I really believed it.

I browse, pausing on a forlorn blue spine. *Lonely Planet: India.* I open it. My card to him is still inside the cover. He must have brought it with him when he left our family's house. My eyes fill. I tuck the book under my arm.

There are some of his small plain black notebooks. More of his jottings. He annotated constantly, for his eyes only, in those faux Moleskines. Forbidden territory, they were, until his death. Now ours for the reading. I still feel like I'm intruding.

He was shorter on resources across his last few years on the streets, in cells, between hostels. Any scraps of paper had to do. Thanks to Bee, I have these too. Turns out, the innards of his notebooks are a wild ride. A tumult of cuttings, maps, drawings, definitions, dates, quotes, facts, fiction:

you can observe a lot by watching – Yogi Bear

jellyfish – sglefrod môr

the realm of the living has a lot to recommend it

never try to nail a blancmange to a pane of glass

khaki is Persian for dust

people, really

we are all strong enough to bear the misfortune of otters

Since when were otters tragic figures? I google the words. It's a quote. Oh, *others*. His handwriting was hit and miss.

I turn the page and come face to face with my own scrawl, diagonal on a torn corner of *The Independent*. Friday 19 November 2010. Back when they still went to print. Slivers of French lyrics, by the looks of it. I wonder why he kept it. He and I would have been in the car in France, somewhere or other in an overcast Pas-de-Calais. Him driving, me trying to pin down a song being played on Cheeeerie FM.

I search the words now. It's from a song by Calogero called 'Prendre Racine' ('Take Root'). Other lines hook me on this second listen, like *avoir peur de revenir* (being scared to return). And yet, fear and tiredness aside, here I am in reverse gear, dredging memories and channelling Yogi Bear. I watch and observe. Surreal, my dad's end, though apt. Surprising only to those who believe in fairy tales.

When I come back downstairs, my eyes are slightly damp. The others look at my face and I'm flustered by the idea that they know I just cried. I pride myself on keeping my composure, even on the day after my dad died. I realise this is not normal.

~

Tomorrow is New Year's Eve. I am leaving Cardiff shortly, heading home to Hebden. I don't want to outstay my welcome at Milno's. Besides, I want to be back with Ash and the kittens. There's an hour until my train departs.

First, Bee and I have to stop by the hostel where our dad spent his last year. It's where his things might be, if he has any. It's around the corner from Cardiff Central. Just down from the Magic Roundabout, between town and Cardiff Bay.

We slip below the bridge. The VW logo looms, signalling the dealership's forecourt where our dad lay dead a few nights ago. I guess he was passing through. There's a one-way sign and expired directions for a youth hostel, marked by a tree and a tent. It's been repurposed for the homeless. I think of the many tents in town, still. My dad knew all about them.

I suddenly remember a tweet I saw just before I left for Melbourne. January, 2019. A councillor posted a picture of herself stood in front of tents on Queen Street. She's wearing lipstick in her photo, wrapped warm in a coat and thick red scarf. The ground behind her is wet.

Tear down these tents, she demanded.

I had been at school with her. She was in the year above and lived just behind Milno. She walked to school on her own. We smiled at her sometimes, but it seemed to us that she had a permanent scowl. 'Moody Cow', we secretly called her. She stood by her words about the tents, and I stand by mine.

Outside the hostel, Bee stays in the car. I linger in the glassy foyer while the reception staff look for the manager. Freshly painted pillars alternate with cheery, cautionary, cheery, cautionary posters. A whiteboard shares the day's meals. I can wait in a separate room, I'm told. A staff member sits beside me. She's around my age.

'Did you know my dad?' I ask. She tears up.

'Oh yeah, such a nice guy, full of banter,' she wipes her face with a sleeve. 'He'd try to sneak in with a bottle of something and we'd say, "What've you got there then, Mike?" and he'd laugh and tell us it was just a bit of squash.'

I crinkle my eyes. 'Sounds about right.'

I want to show her that I know what he was like. I feel so ashamed to be this prodigal daughter. She must wonder where the hell I've been. I pull my mask higher up my nose.

She fiddles with her ID and goes on, 'He'd rattle away in French, he would, and we'd have no clue what he was on about.'

I raise an eyebrow. 'Huh, I mean, he did do classes on Monday nights, before.'

Her eyes glisten again with a grief that seems rawer than mine, than his own child's.

'He was the best dad,' I add, 'until he wasn't. How did he spend this Christmas, do you know?'

She frowns. 'Ah, I'm not sure, sorry. I wasn't on that shift.'

A short, sandy-haired manager appears in the doorway, brisk and bristly.

'I cannot allow you to enter his room without police authorisation.'

I stand up. 'Oh, um, I'm his daughter. Are you sure?'

She keeps the door open with her arm and barks, 'I cannot allow it.'

I assume she's right and thank them both for their time.

Bee drops me at the station. There's no crime scene there this time. I pass the ticket barriers, climb the steps to the platform, and board my train. No hurried online searches for news, no chance now of near-misses.

I change at Manchester, walking fast across the city to get from Piccadilly to Victoria. I walk past men and women lying with duvets in doorways, past some who are crouched beside rucksacks. I see him in every shadowy doorway. When I step off the train at Hebden, the air is cooler and clearer. It makes me feel piercingly alive. In the car park, Ash is waiting to drive me home. Danny rings. He has written something that he reads to me on the phone:

I remember all the times we spent as a happy family going on holidays all of us when we went to the pub and the footy when you me and my sisters went swimming together over the Uhw when we went to france when we went on road trips in the car when we were all a happy family and spent happy memories happy times you changed into a different person when the alcohol took over your body you started getting into trouble with the courts and the police I hope you can be remembered as a good father I hope you are at peace and rest with god and Jesus I will always miss you everyday and night it feels very lonely most of the time now I am always gonna think of you It is not the same without you around anymore

RIP Rest in peace

I remember all the times we spent as a happy family going on holidays all of us when we went to the pub and the footy when you me and my sisters went swimming together over the Uhw when we went to france when we went on road trips in the car when we were all a happy family

and spent happy memories happy times you changed into a different person when the alcohol took over your Body you started getting into trouble with the courts and the poLice I hope you can be remembered as a good father I hope you are at peace and rest with god and Jesus

I will always miss you every day and night it feeLs very LoneLy most of the time now I am aLways gonna think of you It is not the same without you around anymore

RiP Rest in Peace

I want to go home

It is early in the New Year. January, 2022. The sky is a deep, rich blue. I make a cup of tea: Clipper teabag, Yorkshire water, soy milk, stir. My mum would be horrified. I take my mug, along with two armfuls of miscellaneous items, up to my desk in the attic.

I open the skylight, amplifying the birdsong from the beech woods, and sift through photos of my dad's prison notes. They're pencilled diary entries, trembling with so-be-it sobriety. I think of something that the hostel staff member said to me as I was leaving.

'Alcohol is the worst drug,' she said, shaking her head as she opened the door for me. 'Kills you if you go on, and can kill you if you stop.'

When my dad forecast *a different world* for me in 2010, the night I got into Oxford, I could never have imagined this different a world for him.

It was a short prison sentence, four weeks reduced to two weeks, at the very start of 2021. Exactly one year ago. He began last January in a cell and didn't live to see the end of December.

New Year's Day, he wrote. *First full day in prison.*

'Two'ed' with A. Cell 3-6.

Good evening with the 'cleaners' on the 2nd floor. Got a haircut from A + then had nice shower.

Cell search – 'we've been spun'.

The Boys weren't out on the 2nd floor tonight so I got banged up at about 7.00pm.

Weetabix with water. Eating rice krispies with no milk.

I want to go home.

His handwriting wobbles in places. He grew obsessed with the tasks he was given: painting the walls of cells, rails, toilets. Staff had to drag him away. Perhaps it was an effort to lose himself in repetitive activity, a skill of his. Or maybe there was more to it, reaching back to his dad, a painter-decorator all his life and, by then, eighteen months dead. My dad kept seeing his dad and Danny in there.

Hallucination – Dad.

Hallucination – Danny. Danny in trouble. Massive panic attack – couldn't stand up properly.

Read a bit of Oscar + Lucinda – madman next door shouting all night.

A prisoner had hanged himself in that cell recently + A had seen the police arrive + the corpse being taken away in a body bag.

He had been convicted of arson. S said it was freezing in there. The windows were open. A said he could light a camp fire to keep warm.

I'm smiling. Why am I smiling? Who on earth was he even writing this for? He was scathing about another cellmate. Never was one for sharing space.

window warrior shouting – through crack in door – out of window [monopolises TV – WWE – gets excited – terrible rap/hiphop music – dances along – hates me touching it for MOTD/University Challenge/arts programmes]

'it's shit we're not watching it' – The House of Games 6.00 BBC2 my favourite programme
Bullying oh
    oh
    oh
    oh

Sunday lunch – ate it in 2 mins } sucking fingers + thumbs burping farting + taking a piss while I was still eating [tried to flush his chicken bones down the toilet – unsuccessfully] no curtain around toilet. Lack of any privacy at all when defecating

turning light off when I'm reading + he's lying on bottom bunk watching rubbish TV
knows I'm Jumpy + shouts + bangs beds to shred my nerves FOR NO REASON
he thinks it's funny (No Empathy)

I picture the scene, how my dad felt he wasn't supposed to be there. He drunk-drove through my entire childhood, and that wasn't even why he was locked up. He had broken one of the restraining orders, this time by going to Nan's. Not that prison did him any good. Like most people there, I guess, he needed psychologists, not prison officers.

I turn to the pages where he scripted phone calls, graphite dress rehearsals, as if a conversation was by now too difficult for him to improvise. He made his requests to Bee, the only one of us who would respond.

Conversation with Bee
Bee. How are you? I hope that you and the family are OK. Any news? I desperately need you to send me some money here so that I can make calls to my criminal solicitor and my divorce lawyer about hearings to take place in the next few days, the first is tomorrow I believe. I also need to speak to my accountant ... I also need to pay for some items which are not provided free here. £100 would be very useful. I can assure you that you will get a refund [or you could ask Nan to do the transfer if you are too busy today.] I really need it today if possible. You need to go on www.gov.uk/send-prisoner-money + put in my full name [redacted] and my prison number [redacted] and cell no. [redacted]. Not sure if it will ask for my d.o.b. but just in case it's [redacted]. Love to you, Danny, Sophie and Mum. I miss you all.

At that point my mum and he had spent months trampling on each other in those vicious divorce proceedings. He hadn't reached out to me in years. I believe him, though, of course. He never stopped loving us. We never stopped loving him. It's just the way it was.

The official prison papers are merciless:

Tick which emergency pack you require:
(One application per request).
Vape Oils: £3.99 (1 x 3pack)
Grocery Pack: £5.73* (1 Only) ✓
Pin Credit: (Up to £10.00)

*Correct as of 10/07/2020

There's his tick and, below it, his signature. So familiar, forever scribbled on my school planners and trip permission slips. Here, it sits above this:

FOR WING SO TO COMPLETE
Does the above prisoner meet the required criteria and are sufficient spends available?
YES – Send to finance.
NO – Application Rejected. Return to Prisoner.

No one completed it. I picture my dad trying to swallow dry rice krispies and wonder if I wish I had known. I scroll back to this time in my camera roll and find a photo of our fruit bowl fleshed out richly with plums. I swallow, flicking faster through the pages.

They gave me milk, tea + snacks. Spoke to Bee to thank her for sending the £100.

I exhale. Another official paper grabs me. It has blanks in place of answers:

Dear [redacted],

Due to unforeseen circumstances you will not be seen by a Dyfodol (substance misuse) Caseworker at this time.

Primary substance: _____

Please find enclosed information on services and support you can access if you want to change or stop your substance use in the community. Hopefully you can utilise this time in custody to your advantage by maintaining abstinence from substances.

Community agency: _____

Also attached is harm reduction information about the risks associated with your substance use.

Best regards,
Dyfodol Team – Substance Misuse

Dyfodol means *future* in Welsh. My dad's future lasted less than a year from then.

I come across a mind-map of his, titled *Problems outside this prison*, where he plans his route onwards and upwards for his release.

Tax   Debts   need new laptop + phone
how much do I owe 3?   HEARING – NMO
when I am well rebuild relationship with Danny
need to be close to him when I get out
French house finances
Tax + insure car
HEARING – drunk + disorderly
speak to mum – is that OK? I need all my things from there
Financial Remedy Proceedings in Divorce
getting possessions back from Cargo
Exercise =
sleep
Stop drinking
Eat well
long walks
Get out in nature
where do I live?

~

There are other prison papers. *Distraction – Your Weekly Activity Pack*, which my dad repurposed to further his television education. A lifelong habit. Come Monday nights, we were hushed while he perched studiously on the settee, pencil and notebook in hand, for *University Challenge*. His weekly lecture, Paxman as Professor. I read his frantic scribbles across the activity pack, blue ink scrawled in every inch of free space around the bold black text.

longest distance swum underwater = 177m
(nearly 4 lengths of an Olympic pool!)

This fog is so thick I can't see my own cataracts

Hilarious Homophones!

on a piano there are 16 fewer black keys than white keys

New World monkeys have prehensile tails
Old World monkeys (Africa etc) don't have tails

Positive and Negative self-talk

Fate is not an eagle – it creeps like a rat

Nothing prepared me for this kind of habitat

RENOVATIO – Latin for rebirth

he can be temperamental
50% temper 50% mental

Issue 6 – Answers

Pasternak means parsnip in Russian

affineur – someone you pay to mature your cheese

exposition of the colour cerulean in Devil Wears Prada

What don't you like about the pack?

The Danish astronomer Tycho Brahe
owned a tame moose in his castle.
It died after getting drunk and falling
down the stairs. T.B. had a metal nose.
He lost his real nose in a duel – cut off by a sword.

I must write because I have something personal to say.
A heartbreaking journey

See you next week

the 3 Horae in Ancient Greece were the goddesses of seasons

Elsewhere my dad plunges into himself, his bewildered mind and panting body. He is self-pitying, self-everything. I'm not sure how I feel about it.

> *Clinical depression, anxiety attacks, passing out, agitation, chronic insomnia, claustrophobia ... all caused by breakdown of my marriage, losing my job (end of August 2019), being kicked out of my house, being attacked on 21 Dec, robbed of my laptop, arrested.*

Covid
breathless, gasping for air, chronic fatigue, pains in stomach and feet | Long Covid

> *I need to get out of here. This is a mad house. I have a constant base level of anxiety. This place is making a bad situation worse – for everyone. I will be a complete wreck by the time I come out. I feel that this isn't happening – that it's just some kind of dream/hallucination*

The door shuts on me + my heart races + my head spins. I need to be outdoors – I am refreshed by the sea, the fields, the woods, the birds, the sky, the weather. Nature – I find it soothing. Couldn't even stay in my house/office for long

Meditations of Don Quixote: 'I am I + my surroundings + if I do not protect them I do not protect myself.'

Death comes to me like a ghost in these nightmares – cold + wet. I shrink away from it + I cry out. I am startled by the noise + wake up. I have got to get out – put some smart clothes on, meet my younger daughter + get a hug from her + work from there

I just need silence sometimes. I need privacy. Have you seen inside the cell. We had to defecate in full view of each other. No curtain or any other screen – inhumane

Order made that I don't go to her house until 7 Jan 2021 but I have been there 3 times since in breach of the Order + I find myself in prison. Never went inside. Second two times didn't even knock the door

Tried to get accommodation at the Huggard Centre but initially they could offer me nothing so I slept on the street with a tatty sleeping bag. Always felt in danger

Did spend a few peaceful/dry/warm nights at the Cargo, Bute Street. Relative bliss but unceremoniously kicked out + they still have my stuff. Back on the street – tent on 'Island' in Callaghan Square – where I had been doing £80m company deals a year or so earlier. Spectacular fall from grace

Not streetwise – too trusting – other homeless people targeting me to get money bags stolen at Huggard Centre Attempt to steal my wallet Punched in the face (black + blue cut on back of my head). Laptop gone when I came to

Police arrived. Too late. I wanted to go to hospital – concussion? – but they took me to the police station. When I arrived I remember asking whether this was the hospital + one of the coppers said yes, it is. They locked me in a cell. 2 panic attacks in the morning – now panic is so severe it can render me unconscious. Deadly combination is bad news or terrible frustration + being locked in a small space

Living in a leaky tent

Anxiety attacks
– can be so severe I pass out
– drink helps a bit

In Barry, after some very unpleasant incidents in Cardiff (with other homeless people)
fed up of violence
threat of violence
Didn't sleep a wink previous night
someone prowling outside tent smashing bottles 1–2am

Emotional/crying wanted to be on my own in a safe place

One minute I am trying to sleep in an underpass (hardly used) a long way from my mum's I have been able to sleep there but that was in a sleeping bag when I was able to keep it dry it was stolen yesterday along with a bag of clothes

I didn't drink too much yesterday 3/4 bottle of wine – it makes you feel cold + hinders sleep

Covid symptoms pain everywhere

Chronic fatigue
Breathless

Gravitated to mum's

My breathing has become shallow, fast. I set aside my dad's words and put on my merry wellies, then plod into the woods beside our home. I can't take for granted the nature he longed for. I remind myself: I am free I am free I am free.

the things we would do

I get many calls in the days after my dad's death. Mainly it's officials asking me the same questions.

'Did he die at home or in hospital?' That one comes up a lot.

'Neither,' I reply. 'He was found in a car park.'

They never know quite what to say to that.

The sky is clear. Ash and I are visiting abbey ruins at the edge of the Yorkshire Dales, where decay comes with a hefty entrance fee. I think of other kinds of decay, him slumped in an underpass.

I photograph puddles reflecting rubble and big black birds. I think they're ravens. Or crows. My dad would know. There's no ceiling, only open air. The bright chill is winning its fight against my winterwear.

He's been dead a week now. He's never not in my mind. I drink hot Vimto on a bench, cold sunshine on my forehead. Halfway up a hill, my phone vibrates in my coat. I hurry out of my gloves and apologise for my breathlessness.

'Inconclusive, the post-mortem was, love,' trills Nat from Cardiff Coroner's. '50–60 per cent are.'

They need to test his body further. Liver, kidneys, lungs, blood, heart. We discuss tissue retention and she lists four options.

I don't hesitate. 'Number four, donate afterwards.' I feel quite sanctimonious about this.

Nat tells me all that stuff about his hostel room is rubbish. I ring again, but the manager doubles down on her refusal. I wonder if she hates me, if our family has been a pain for her.

'I'll be in touch,' she mutters.

I ring the hostel a few more times over the following days, at last getting through.

'I'll come in on Tuesday,' I say.

She snaps, 'I'll try to make the necessary arrangements.'

My phone's off the hook at the moment. I need to catch up on my correspondence. For this I favour Ash's study, now my unofficial death office. A better spot for all this admin than our kitchen. Another call. This time it's Huw, with the mountainous voice. He's in a Welsh choir, *wrth gwrs*, of course. I enjoy hearing from him more than I should, given he's the funeral director.

'I can do as much or as little as you want. I am completely at your service,' Huw sings.

I ask him to talk me through it. 'I'm new to this,' I say, meaning the handling of corpses.

The littlest, it turns out, would be a case of Huw fetching my dad from the hospital, pending the interim death certificate, then placing his body in a coffin and taking it to his final resting place.

'I don't know what sort of state he'd have been in,' I note, by way of apology. 'He was homeless, you see, and an alcoholic.' Other things too, I want to add.

Huw expresses sympathies and asks if I've given thought to the service.

'Just a small one at the natural burial meadow,' I reply. 'Me, my sister and mum, and his brother and mum.' I start to babble. 'I'll sort a bigger memorial for the end of the month, his birthday, when he'd have turned 56.'

I have to say this, in case Huw thinks no one else loved him. We move on to the question of coffins.

'We'll need to get one ordered asap,' Huw says, 'What with the December delays and people on holidays. And it'll have to be eco, for the natural burial meadow,' he reminds me.

'Hmmm, I know this might sound strange,' I venture, 'but are there any we could paint?'

Without missing a beat, Huw suggests a white canvas coffin that he can drop off to me and pick up a few days later. I request the earliest possible burial date. We're working around Steve's trip to Tenerife. Nan is keen to see her remaining son get some winter sun.

The days go fast, busy, until I have to leave Hebden for Cardiff again. On the train I write a poem for the burial. It comes easily:

See the beauty, you said to me,
As we hurtled towards the sea,
Through bird-burble scrub, up and up,
The December-Sunday dunes,
Higher still, into white-horse skies,

You five paces ahead to guide
My happy-green childhood steps.

See the beauty, you said to me,
As we sauntered up southern scree,
Steep slopes, ropes and waterfalls
Reserved, we were told, for professionals,
We laughed, of course, and ventured forth,
Chuffed to bits with risk and reward,
Exploring til dusk's chorus called.

See the beauty, you said to me,
As you handed us paints and dreams,
Scenes in Mametz, warm bread, and chess,
Kippers, lists, and avocets,
Fishboats bobbing, nonsense jottings, the comedy of theology,
Our old mate, Alice, memorialising from memory,
Jam pots, missions from God, rat bones, and the Minute Waltz.

See the beauty, you said to me,
As you conjured spires and joie de vivre,
Then spiralled into your own world
While I headed off into adulthood,
Circling the same drain until our final exchange,
Well-refreshed, you were, on my work lunch-break,
One last look, longer-lasting heartache.

See the beauty, didn't you say,
Or did you briefly lose your way,
Muttering French in gutters,
Glugging 'squash', you'd chuckle,
Well, I suspect you saw embers til the end,
Wild-minded, truly free
To seek beauty wherever you wanted it to be.

See the beauty, you said to me,
And I see it, still, at your burial,
Fresh air, trees, all you need
For a life well lived, I know you'd agree,
So: 'pending', we write, as to the cause,
You evade explanation,
A farewell entirely yours.

See the beauty, you say to me,
Your forever Will and legacy,
And my reply, in truth, will be:
We love you unconditionally.

This time I sleep at Grandma's, like I did when I was small, in need of peace and quiet. Her home glows and glitters with lamps, mirrors, *pili-palas* (butterflies), paintings by Uncle Glyn. He and Aunty Meryl live in another beautiful magpie's nest in Taff's Well. Grandma offers me Prosecco and at first I reject it, then the second time I accept. I'm not sure why. Politeness, I like to think, rather than desire.

In my late teens, I migrated to hers when things weren't so good at ours. Once I was alone there and heard the front door open. Out of the window I saw my dad's car and I hid upstairs, still and silent until I was sure he'd left. I crept downstairs and found a bouquet in her hallway. An apology. And there was me thinking he had come to hurt me.

Bee drives me to the hostel again. The person at reception tries to get hold of the manager on duty. To my right, a pale woman is leaning against a wall. Around my age, late twenties. She's telling someone down the phone that she has changed, that she loves them so, so much. A pause, then she breaks down, her face and body crumpling. I look at the ceiling to steel my eyes. It's been years since

I was the person at the other end of the line, pretending his words could no longer reach me.

The receptionist tells me to wait outside. Health and safety. The tone is totally different this time. As I head out I hold open the door for a thin, jittery man and smile at him, as if I know what I'm doing here. Bee has left the engine running. This place is familiar to her. She had to come here a lot over the past year. I perch on the passenger seat, watching a huddle of people nearby. Bee points out those she recognises. After a minute or so, two women raise their voices. She locks the car doors.

Embarrassed, I turn. 'Mate, they could hear that, you know.'

She shrugs, absent-mindedly wet-wiping the dashboard. A tall, broad man ambles over.

'Security,' Bee nods. 'Nice guy. Always helped when Dad went AWOL.'

He ushers everyone onwards with easy words and warm gestures. They hush and disperse. A knock on the car window jolts us. Bee turns down the radio and tucks the wet-wipes into her cup-holder. A staff member hops from one foot to the other.

'Sorry to keep you waiting, girls, and for your loss. So sorry. Why don't you park up, come on in.'

We re-hook our masks as she leads us into a wing with a fob. We pull up at Room 107. She negotiates with a ring heavy with keys. I commit this to memory, Room 107, then examine the door. Thick, walnut. Silver handle. She puts a key to the lock. My stomach clenches.

It doesn't open. She's reshuffling, muttering more condolences. How shocked they were, how popular he was. I pick my lip.

'Uh, wasn't he 103?' Bee offers, eventually. I glance at her with an unspoken, pointed look ('What the hell took you so long?').

'What am I like, course he was. Mind of a sieve, me,' the woman chuckles.

We make courtesy laughter noises and follow her two doors down. Thick, walnut. Silver handle. Identical. She steps into the room and switches on the overhead lights. I blink, then almost slip on an unopened envelope. *Season's Greetings* from the staff.

The room is dim, battleship grey, and stinks of stale smoke. The stench throbs in the airless room, choking my throat. I make out the shapes of a desk, bookshelves, two bunkbeds, a bedside table, a red armchair, all of it littered in stuff.

She hands me a wad of bin bags before leaving. 'I'll come see how you're doing in a bit.'

She's gone. I spin on my left heel, trying to take it in. I recognise nothing of his.

'Was this definitely his room?'

'Yeah, I've been here,' Bee says, picking up some of the clutter on the desk.

'But he didn't smoke?'

'He did, towards the end. Anyway, you can tell it's him. The jams.'

She holds up a bowl overflowing with condiments. Jams of four flavours: apricot, raspberry, strawberry, blackcurrant. Plus mint sauce, salt, butter, ketchup. I look further and see at least fifty sugar sachets, scattergun.

Echoes, echoes. 'Take what you can,' the room whispers. He always made us grab as much as we could carry from buffets. We lined our pockets and filled plastic bags with our hauls.

I look further. Boxes of batteries cascade onto the brown carpet. Heaps of clothes, none I recognise, smother the four unmade beds. Grey tops, black joggers, a camouflage hoody. I turn to the shelf. Piles of crime fiction. 'Couldn't make it up,' I say to Bee.

Then I notice two lemons. *Lemons. Tin foil. Cat food*, he used to write at the top of every shopping list. I register only now the three empty red wine bottles gloating unashamedly in the crook of the armchair. Christ, I start to believe my dad really was here.

Bee holds up a 6x4 photo of us. 'I gave him this,' she says, eyes welling. 'He kept it.'

I smile and study it. 'Of course,' I reply, as if I still know anything for certain.

I open the window a crack and begin to bag up clothes. Not to take, just to create some breathing space. I realise I'm nervous about touching his stuff. Should I have brought gloves? The thought mortifies me. Gloves? I'm his daughter. I was his daughter.

I push open the bathroom door. More mess, heaps of excess. Deodorants, shampoos, shaving gels are strewn across the tiles and cabinet. Too many to count. He must have scooped them from anywhere and everywhere he could. I can feel his anticipation of scarcity. A hangover, I guess, from the poverty of generations past.

I asked Nan about her parents, not long back. She told me a ship rope had snapped and hit her dad, my dad's grandfather. He was a seaman. The rope smacked his body full force. He lost a kidney. It cut short his movements. He could no longer get out into the open water. From then, he could only work the Docks, earning a pittance to feed his five kids. I wonder if here, too, in this bathroom, were the burns of that rope.

I meet my eyes in the bathroom mirror, then take out my phone and photograph it. Then the jams, armchair, bunkbeds. There's an icy hardness to this, my obsession with documenting everything. My fear of forgetting. Another mode of anticipating scarcity, loss, the deterioration of my mind and memories.

I look at Bee. She's standing, tearful, ready to leave. We can't have been here for more than ten minutes. She shows me what she's taking: his decades-old grey Gillette razor and battered old Roberts radio, sellotaped, grimy, loved.

'God, as if he still had those.' I shake my head. 'So are they thinking we'll tidy all this, or...?'

'No, they'll do that,' Bee says.

'Shall we head off then?'

'Yep.'

As we leave, she slings an artwork under her arm. I turn it towards me. 'Uh, it's shit. No way is it one of his.'

'Nah, he probs found it,' Bee replies.

'You don't actually want it?'

'Why not, take what you—'

'Don't say it.' I shut the door behind us.

A few hours later, I'm eating microwaved samosas and sipping Prosecco with Grandma. She's in slippers and a dressing gown. She seems far older now as well. I get a text from Huw. *Be with you in 20.* I tell her I'm expecting a delivery. When her dog barks, I go to the window and see a black Mercedes. Huw gets out, clad in a dark suit. Bit funerary for my liking. I wave, apprehensive, as he slides the coffin lid from the boot. I lead him to a room where I assume no one's likely to bump into it.

In my head I'm cracking up a bit at what my dad would think of me sneaking this past his mother-in-law. I ask Huw to let me know the cost of his time and petrol. He won't hear of it. 'Complimentary. I'm here to help.'

I ask Bee to bring paints and brushes from the house where we grew up. In the meantime, I take a pencil and sketch the details I have to include by law: our dad's name, age, and date of death.

'Uh what the fuck?' Bee's in the doorway. 'It's an actual coffin.'

She's staring at the soon-to-be 'artwork', as I prefer to term it, laid on the carpet.

'Well, the lid of it.' I stand and wipe my hands on my jeans. 'Did you pick up the stuff?'

She dumps a Tesco bag on the rug and tips it sideways.

'Amazing.' I pick up a brush and inspect the bristles. 'I made a start in pencil. We have to write this bit, Huw said.'

'Right.' She doesn't look up, scrolling her phone.

We go back in to sit with Grandma. Bee tops up our glasses. A while later, our mum drops in with Danny. We have two days until the artwork's deadline.

I think fast and go carefully. 'Danny, can you help me?' Our mum makes a warning sound. She doesn't want him involved in any of this.

'I need words to remember Dad,' I say. 'What comes to mind for you?'

He reels off a bunch. No questions asked. Without hesitation, repetition, or deviation.

'Mackerel Chagall fruit salad Grémont's lime-green Kawasaki.' He takes a breath. 'University Challenge The Archers Merthyr Mawr Jacksons Spade.'

His stream of consciousness doesn't end for several minutes. I grab fifty or so from mid-air, typing them into my Notes app. There were so many we hadn't thought of. Bee's jaw has dropped. Danny doesn't stop until I lock my phone.

'Do you want to see it?' I ask. 'The artw—?'

Our mum interrupts. 'It's getting late.'

I'm already on my feet. 'D'you want to?' I say to Danny.

He gets up too. 'Yes.'

I stay in casual mode, chatting as I lead him to the artwork.

'You could add some of your words,' Bee says, kneeling to show him how.

It's like those Saturdays when we'd come downstairs to a slab of wood on the kitchen table, swept in by the morning tide along with acrylics, gouache, netting. And our dad on the shoreline, under the skylight, waving brushes in a torn pink shirt. 'Let's paint!'

He was March-hare mad and fearless, on the surface of it. He's here tonight in spirit. The three of us work side by side, peacefully. At some point our mum tiptoes in and watches from a stool in the corner. Later she texts me:

It was heartwarming seeing you all together but equally heartbreaking knowing why you were. You are his legacy and he would be so proud of you all.

He and Danny were inseparable once. For Danny's 16th, our dad wrote a poem to *the greatest hero ever known*. He wove in their inside jokes and reminisced about fishing trips. He closed it by wishing for his son, someday, the *biggest catch* he could imagine: *peace of mind*.

I see us in my dad's notes from while he was homeless, once he no longer saw us. He reminded himself of phone calls with Danny long ago:

We spoke about all the things Danny had been doing + the things we would do when the pandemic was over. He would always end by saying: 'Love you Dad.'

> *Don't want to talk to anyone except my children – but only my ~~elder~~ younger daughter keeps in touch.*

I pause on his strike through *elder*, the notion that, in that moment, he thought of me. He used to call me Elder Daughter sometimes. I learned recently that elders are known as the 'Judas tree'. From Anglo-Saxon 'aeld', meaning fire. Olden-days people said if you burned elder wood you'd see the devil. There's another theory I like better: if planted near home, elders keep the devil away.

I ask a family member when they last saw my dad. I'm sat on Grandma's sofa, cross-legged, finishing a mug of hot chocolate. They had bumped into him two weeks ago in town, hovering by the black railings opposite Ashton's. He had been in the hostel almost a year by then. He was eating cockles from a polystyrene tub, malt vinegared, white peppered. He must have scrounged some cash from the divorce lawyer who was charging him to access his own money.

After a minute or so of talking, my dad's eyes and feet meandered. They watched him hand over a tenner to a woman sat on the ground with a cardboard plea. They caught up and my dad turned, surprised, then shrugged. 'Well, I know what it's like, don't I, not to have a roof over my head.'

That was just two weeks before he stopped breathing. I easily might never have known it, this paragraph from a chapter of his life that I only have second-hand. Another near-miss among countless misses. The price of estrangement. I feel greedy, wanting to pocket glimpses from these lost years despite having cut off contact. I don't deserve them. I treasure it, remembering this scene in my imagination as if I was there. I guess I did see his decades of generosity to me.

On the evening before the burial, I head out for dinner with Bee and Lloyd. We walk on impulse into Cardiff's new branch of The

Ivy. It's ideally distracting with its flamboyant décor and dishes. We have a nice time. Our dad would be happy for us. He likewise prioritised pleasure.

And then it's Wednesday 12 January 2022. We're burying our dad today.

It's 7:42 am. I take a photo of dawn from Grandma's eastward bedroom. The sun is low, bashful among the trees. Clear orange meets clear blue. It's the sky I had dared to dream of for this day in the natural burial meadow. I had willed it to be dry, heart set on sunshine. I review the photo. It's smeared. She needs to clean her windows.

Downstairs,
tea,
Weetabix.

Yes, somehow I can trace the shape of this again.

Huw calls to check how I'm doing. I stand by Grandma's dressing table and reassure him I'm fine. He tells me that he'd had a conversation with a friend who had known my dad back in the day. The friend had reached out to Huw after hearing the news. A lawyer, he had crossed paths with my dad over the years and didn't realise he had a drinking problem. The friend told Huw that he had actually envied my dad, the man who 'had it all, beautiful wife, lovely kids, top job, great home.' He was shocked that the man he knew could have died so young, homeless and alone.

Afterwards, I put on a jacket I'm borrowing from Grandma. I take another photo in a mirror that beams light, splicing me down the middle. She and I have the same taste, not that it's to everyone's. It's a half-collared button-up thing plastered in giant pink flowers and wild green leaves. I spot my mum's car outside. I hurry to brush on mascara and lipstick, then brace myself. She comes in. I look at her face and see her eyes are shiny.

'Noticed you wrote a poem as well,' I say. 'It's awesome, wanna read it out?'

'God no,' she squawks, horrified.

'Okydoky, I'll do it.' I speak in a tone more suited to shallower occasions. I was raised with irreverence, after all.

She looks at my face now, too, and I don't know what she sees, because all she says is, 'You're not putting on any make-up?'

Bee arrives and laughs at me. 'You look like a priest.'

I bring my palms into a mock-prayer stance, intoning, 'We are gathered here today...'

Lloyd drives us to the natural burial meadow, midway between Cardiff and Barry: my dad's two homes. Danny is at home with his carer. Our mum thought it would be too much for him. We're very early for once. Turns out Nan and Steve are even earlier. Then Huw is early too, but more of the socially acceptable kind. I introduce him to everyone in the car park like he's an old friend. Lloyd hugs Bee and returns to the car.

We keep on our sunglasses, Bee and I. They're a trusty shield, usually. Less so today for my sister. Her fake tan means the tears are streaming telltale trails as white as ash. I only let her know afterwards, when we could all do with a laugh.

The speakers hum our first song, Fairport Convention's 'Who Knows Where The Time Goes?' Sandy Denny sings of birds leaving, then returning in spring after the storms of winter. 'I have no fear of time,' her voice ripples. Huw's pallbearers bring over my dad to be lowered into the earth. Bee heads alone into a nearby grove. 'A class act,' my dad would say of all these massive trees. He likes ones that make a statement. That present tense was an accident. Let's keep it, for now.

His coffin sings with colour, life, his refrains. Inside it— I can't think of it, him. My throat tightens but my voice is sturdy as I begin speaking. I have a structure, not quite a script, in a small plain black notebook. One of his. I couldn't bear the idea of a stranger sending him off. Nan and my mum hold each other. Steve stands motionless, stoic, looking at our words on the coffin.

For the service, I nestle poems between songs. 'Sea-Fever', John Masefield. 'Shipbuilding', Elvis Costello. 'The Minute Waltz', Chopin. My poem, my mum's poem. 'Reasons to Be Cheerful, Pt. 3', Ian Dury and the Blockheads. I'm not thinking about the proximity of my dad's body below me. I am but I'm not. I can't.

I opted out of seeing him after he died. There was an irreversibility to it that unnerved me. I know it can help some with closure. For our family, I doubt it. Pummelled purple by tarmac, polluted by cheap red (and cigarettes, so I hear), a person withered where once he had lived. I'm not saying goodbye to that guy, and I already said goodbye to the dad I had known three years ago.

'Did you not cry at all?' my mum asks, staring at me, as we walk back to the car.

We all go for coffee at the garden centre in Wenvoe. The conversation is civilised. We talk about weightless things, like Steve's upcoming Tenerife trip. I'm starving, I realise. Next, Lloyd chauffeurs us over for lunch in Cardiff Bay before I get my train back up to Hebden.

I'm finding it kind of wild that no one around us has any idea that we've just buried our dad. I'm thinking I need to be extra kind to everyone I meet, in case they've also just buried their dads. Bee eyes the ugly fake plant on the table.

'Don't,' Lloyd says.

I'm alarmed to learn that she is developing a low-key interest in petty theft.

'It's minging,' I sigh. 'Why would you even consider taking it? Wait, don't answer that.'

I don't think about any of it until I'm on Platform 3 at Cardiff Central, still sheltered by my sunglasses. Alone at last, I cry. On the train, I read some of my dad's notebooks. In one, he left a poem incomplete. *The Wreck of the Hesperus.* He had come to an abrupt halt after *Down came the storm and smote amain / The vessel in its strength;*

I look it up and finish scribing the last verses. A joint effort. I smile. Diving for pearls.

we do not get any younger

Back in Hebden, I yelp with excitement as we step out for our morning walk. A snowdrop has emerged in a pot by our front door. A symbol of hope, or is it consolation, I forget. My brain's a bit scattered but I'm keeping a cool demeanour, yelp aside. I check its proper name so I can greet it more civilly tomorrow. *Galanthus*, milk flower.

More sunshine and blue skies. Mid-January. It's supposed to be winter. I wonder where the clouds went. It's a bereavement of lonely, lovely skies. Most lunch-breaks I'm running up on the moors, bolting from my desk. I never really stopped working, to Bee's disdain. The podcast's Slack channel demanded my attention. It's weird how a term for idleness means something so tiringly incessant.

My workplace stalks me around my home. I'm ambushed while I eat and sleep by colleagues who don't believe in leave. The morning after his burial, they reach out to get my input on a comms plan. I stare at the sharp asks in place of condolences. Still, I'd rather be stalked than trapped, static, between a swivel chair and the coldness of a hot desk.

While the weather is playing dumb, my bookshelf knows what's what. It propelled me last night to a memoir, *H is for Hawk*, by a writer whose dad had died. The author, Helen Macdonald, gets a goshawk. My kittens should suffice. At one point she describes another hawker, one who drinks. She describes obliteration of promises and disintegration of selfhood. It rings a bell.

I plan my dad's memorial for the day before his unmet 56th birthday, four weeks after his death. I decide to put a photo of the five of us on the invite. It feels right, despite our splintering. The drinking put distance between him and everyone else as well, not just us. The photo is one we took on self-timer one balmy night in the garden of The Tŷ Mawr. He's in the centre, arms crossed and confident. The four of us lean into him. We're radiant. We're smiling.

There was no question of a funeral, the doom and gloom of it all. We'll say farewell at the seaside, where there's beauty to be seen. People will be coming from as far-flung as Swansea and London, and us, the northern contingent, all descending on Barry Island. I look up our beach hut, number seven. It's red and blue, like a bruise.

The weekend comes. I'm Cardiff-bound for the third time in four weeks after years apart. Ash is loading the car. I'm being useful too, fussing about the kittens' routine. *Just a whirlwind visit*, I text friends. We set off.

As we cross into Wales on the A40, I trundle aloud down memory lane. I am recalling a previous memorial, an excavation of the *Iliad*, that my dad and I went to together in Oxford. Alice Oswald was reciting her poem *Memorial*.

'He had done a tonne of research,' I tell Ash. 'He even brought a poly pocket of website pages he had printed in his office.'

'We went into the lecture theatre and there in the front row was Stephen, you know, my favourite tutor. We sat next to Stephen, my dad and I, and chatted about *Memorial* together.'

I didn't say the next bit, how sitting between them, my dad noting the poet's likely influences, Stephen agreeing with him, I felt a rush of emotion. Even as it was happening, I knew I wouldn't forget that moment. In its way, sort of ethereal. A realisation of our wildest childhood dreams.

'Grief is black,' Oswald recited that day, 'it is made of earth. It gets into the cracks in the eyes. It lodges its lump in the throat.'

My voice cracks slightly as I say to Ash, ten years later, 'We got our copy signed afterwards. She was nice.'

The next morning, I wake early in Cardiff to what looks through the window uncannily like a summer's day. Sunday 30 January 2022. The day of my dad's memorial. We're staying at Milno's. I shower straightaway because, if I know anything, I know about impermanence. No way am I letting this sky get away from me. It's another I had dared to dream of, heart-aching sunshine. I put on one of Grandma's vibrant jackets.

'Can't get over the weather this month,' I say through a mouthful of toast in the kitchen. Milno, Ash, and I are leaning against the countertops, drinking strong black coffee and discussing traffic fines. We head to Barry Island. A place our dad always brought us, the guy who's buried in a meadow eight miles away. His absence is the reason we're all here.

'Wow, this weather hey?' I repeat blandly, affably, to everyone I see.

Bee gets out of the shabby, battered Merc that was once our dad's. I run over and exclaim about the sun. She's raging. She had bought a marquee on Gumtree, anticipating rain. The beach in January was a gamble that paid off. We lug refreshments to the hut.

I'm buzzing with adrenaline, like I used to on the starting line of races. I wonder if people will think I'm dissociating, or in shock, or happy he's gone. Really, I'm just relieved and conflicted about this dry, warm winter morning which I had betted on and which, I imagine, had something to do with him.

We jazz up Grandad's old painting table with colourful cloths then fill vases with daffodils. They fanfare after Steve tips in water from a sandy-feet tap. Life leaps headlong into the air. I take off my jacket. To be honest, it's unseasonably hot. Nan puts out homemade Welsh cakes. There's coffee, tea, juice, croissants, cheese, the works.

Our dad's friends gravitate. I lose count, seventy, seventy-five, eighty … I greet them all with gratitude.

'I'll say a few words in five minutes,' I say to clusters of them every five minutes or so.

I'm holding off, waiting for his mates from college who aren't here yet. I want them to hear it.

A neighbour tears up, recalling her last conversation with him. He arrived at their door, sober, and they spoke for over an hour. He had turned up many times before that, she tells me. In the dark. Drunk. Terrifying her and her husband. I thought he only did that to us.

His old firm's receptionist stops me. 'You've not changed a bit.'

She reminisces, 'Ah your dad, a fantastic dancer, he was. Fantastic. Life and soul of every do.'

We talk of the time when Buena Vista Social Club came to town. The music, laughter, dancing.

'He was dead proud of you going to the jungle, you know,' she says.

'The jungle?'

'In Calais. Told everyone about that, dead proud he was.'

I can't delay much longer. I call out, and people circle around me. Nan comes to my left and chips in ad hoc, like some kind of comedian. A dog sits regally to my right. I have no clue who he's with, but he brings a decorum to proceedings. That is, until liquid trickles down the steps.

I go off-piste from what I had prepared. My dad's tribute evolves, alive and kicking.

'... *As we get older, we do not get any younger*, he used to say. Tomorrow would've been his 56th birthday. I looked up that quote this week for the first time. Turns out it's from a poem by Henry Reed. The next line kind of struck a chord. *Seasons return, and today I am fifty-five*. The age our dad was when he died.'

I go on, 'He loved the sea, in his words, *the taste of the saltwater, the smell, the movement, the moods: calm, tempestuous. Every day is different...*'

I talk for a couple of minutes. People laugh and cry. There's always been *enargeia* in anything that relates to my dad. Extreme vividness. Bright, unbearable reality. Both apply, I think.

I turn my gaze to the water, whose surface-level serenity hides the world's second-biggest tidal range, right here between Wales and England. I think of the red-wine riptide in what was our family home. Those undercurrents took us by surprise and swept off our strongest swimmer. I only knew too late the depths of debt he left behind. I surmise our dad's thirst for other worlds was from all the saltwater he swallowed here in childhood.

My dad's college mates miss the speech. They had a big night and got lost on their way over here.

'They are *hanging*,' Bee observes through her sunglasses.

One of them proudly shows me a certificate that my dad had posted him as a surprise, attesting that Dave did indeed hit three triple twenties in darts. My dad had been the sole witness. He had signed it as a notary public, stamping it with his seal.

Bee and I give out wildflower seeds and *see the beauty* cards for people to keep in their wallets. Everyone tells me how great he was. I let them. It's as true as it's not.

Towards the end I'm approached by my godfather, my dad's best friend from school.

'I—I didn't know,' he says. 'I had no, no idea he was so—'. He trails off.

My mum must have filled him in.

I help him. 'Yeah, I mean, he wasn't in a good way recently. Guessing you've just heard, like, the homelessness and stuff.'

I share a few benign anecdotes, then shrug. 'It wasn't all sad. In some ways he was freer than he'd ever been.'

If freedom is to flee reality, that is.

Once most people have headed off, I sit with Ash and my school friends on the rocks. We eat greasy chips with curry sauce.

'I brought my bikini,' I tell them, laughing. 'I'm serious. Could do, right?'

Could, but don't for now. The sun's drooping, the warmth wilting, and it's time for goodbyes. We decide to drive all the way back up to Hebden. I'm exhausted, but Cardiff isn't home anymore. It's dark by the time we get in. The kittens leap into my lap and snuggle close, purring. I check my phone. Friends' photos, captioned *see the beauty*, are all over my Instagram feed. Once again I'm happy, sad, everything in between.

bewilderment

It's February, my least favourite month, and the weather has turned. It's freezing, wet, windy.

My focus now has to be on legal matters. I'm back and forth, back and forth with lawyers around my working hours. The email chains drain me. I read poetry by Mary Oliver and Alice Oswald to quieten my mind during my rare spare moments. My dad died intestate, that is, without a will. I agree to be administrator of the estate, and learn that he died with liabilities of almost £300,000. He had barely enough to pay these, let alone to live off. I worry that debt played a part in his death.

I recall what my German friend once said at the edge of the Rhein. 'The currency is very strong.'

I corrected him, at the time, with a smile. 'Current, you mean.'

I suspect now that money matters can also drown people. *Not waving, but drowning.*

I ring Bee. She's as shocked as I am. We go in search of his laptop. Turns out it's still being held by the lawyer he hired for the divorce. We retrieve it and trawl his inbox to find out how this happened. It's full of emails with the lawyer's monthly invoices charging him six minutes by six minutes by six minutes.

He was homeless by then, and very vulnerable. She deserted him before the final hearing, to the Judge's disapproval, then quietly had him appoint her as his Power of Attorney. How could he have surrendered his finances to a stranger? A stranger who left his debts to accrue interest, yet sent herself his money until his death. Bills for perusal of documents. Bills for unanswered emails sent to her. Bills for access to his own money, over and over. And then this:

| 18/06/2021 | Telephone call to Clients mother (as requested by client) Clients mother confirmed she was well and asked that we inform Client that she still thinks of him and loves him very much. | 6 | £26.50 |

A nice, round six minutes. £26.50. Another cost of love estranged. I resent the lawyer for this.

I ask South Wales Police if they had any dealings with my dad around this time, when the Power of Attorney was signed. I'm told they had to attend a scene at another law firm the month before. My dad had walked into their reception and made a scene, insisting someone was trying to get into his bank account. I take notes in an orange highlighter, the only pen to hand, as the police officer lists incidents with him, pissed and unhinged, in the weeks around the signing.

I learn, too, that there was no psychological professional with him when he signed over this power. Just a junior employee at the law firm. I assume, but will never know for sure, that he was drunk. It seems unjust, but my attentiveness has come too late. The Solicitors Regulation Authority says it can't help. Nor can the Legal Ombudsman, nor the Office of the Public Guardian. Your dad is dead, they inform me, so there's nothing to be done.

Instead, I text Nan cheery, free notes of love. When all's said and done, my dad's decades of slog left an immaterial inheritance for his kids: little left from making a living, but invaluable lessons on how not to live.

~

It's ten weeks since I heard the news of his death. Early March. I'm alone on a train, heading to Gatwick airport for a work trip with the podcast team. It's pre-dawn, 3°C.

I hear a male voice approaching behind me. I don't catch his words to others over my music, so I assume it's a ticket inspector. I open the obligatory apps: Trainline, Railcard. I take out a headphone and turn as he reaches my seat.

The man has his hood up, rubbing his hands. He looks cold. And then it hits me, the stale smoke throbbing on his clothes. My dad, my dad's airless hostel room. I'm immediately back there. The smell is choking my throat all over again.

He coughs. 'Could you spare any change to help me get off the streets?'

I dip my head, thrown. 'Sorry,' I whisper, with a slight shake of my head.

'I'm sorry to have bothered you,' he replies, and moves on.

For the rest of the journey I wish I had been a better person in that moment. I hate how I responded. I can't shake the feeling that I'm back there in that hostel room. It was the smell that stayed with me long after we had bagged up our dad's belongings. His radio, his razor.

I find my colleagues at check-in and we fly to San José, Costa Rica.

We take a tiny plane to the co-founder's oceanfront compound. We were asked to come for a staff retreat. This place is thought to resemble paradise. *It's a different world now.* I find it quite jarring.

At dawn each day, I do lengths in the pool or run along the bay. One day I cry as I swim, missing Ash. We haven't spent more than a weekend apart since before Australia. I'm not sure why I'm here. It doesn't feel right. Climate justice? I don't think this is it.

One morning, though, I wake up excited about life. My dreams must have been kind to me. I smile as I run, mesmerised by the sun rising from behind the hills. I impulsively walk into the waves in my vest and shorts, and kneel quietly in the warm water. The light casts amber glitter on the ripples. It's cinematic. I wish my dad could see this.

At the start of each day's agenda, we're invited to sit in a circle on a rug and share our 'internal weather'. I stay resolutely upbeat, breezy.

'Pretty sunny today,' I say, daily.

Towards the end of our retreat, the circle is washed away. A colleague begins to cry about a friend who is ill. The display of emotion makes me well up. I try to hold it in, but can't seem to control myself. I never cry in front of people. Another starts to speak, then notices my face and all its noiseless boundless sadness.

'Do you need to—', he says.

'Yup,' I respond, nodding as I stand. I grab a tissue then go to sit on the patio. A colleague brings me a glass of water. I miss Ash even more. I'm not sure where I'm supposed to be, but this isn't paradise to me.

I think of the Nirvana poster. Danny and our dad beside it, laughing at me and Bee, the slowcoaches, dawdling out after a swim, like we had all the time in the world.

~

Two weeks later, I'm back home in Hebden. The kittens have followed me up into the attic, where I prepare tweets and trailers and they busy themselves shredding our monstera. I scrunch old work notes into a ball and hurl it down the stairs. The last unscathed leaf lives a minute more. Well, I'm on my feet now aren't I, and what is it, 10:30? Coffee time. I head to the kitchen, cats at my ankles.

'Quickly, quickly,' I usher them. It's a joke between me and these small friends of mine. There's no hurry. Life is slower-paced these days.

I stoop for an envelope on the doormat. It's addressed to me, with a coroner's stamp. I unseal it as the beans are grinding (yes I've been gentrified) and unfold it while the pourover's dripping (I know). I stop. *Notice of Discontinuance.*

The post-mortem examination has revealed *a natural cause of death.* I stare at this word, *natural.* A fifty-five year old dead on the ground outside a VW dealership is natural, right. Right?

The matter has been discontinued, the letter goes on.

The medical cause of death recorded by the pathologist was:
1 (a) Myocardial Fibrosis
  (b)
  (c)
II

The inconsistency of the *I* and *II* irks me. Silly errors had littered the interim certificate too. I inherited my dad's obsession with details and, though undignified at times, I resent indignity in his dying. Besides, I feel like the field of death should be one where people don't get stuff wrong.

There is no mention of alcoholism. I am stunned, though, that we have any explanation. It seems out of character. My dad was an enigma. I turn the page. One of the kittens freezes at her watering hole, ears pricked at the sound of paper. Her favourite chase. She skitters over and I jostle the certificate, more than tempted. For her, it's all a game.

I think better of it. Instead I sit on the sofa and sip my coffee, searching *myocardial fibrosis* on my phone browser. I click on webpages of words I don't understand, then add *alcoholism* to the search bar.

> *Alcoholic cardiomyopathy is a condition where your heart changes shape because of long-term heavy alcohol use. The changes to your heart's shape cause long-term damage...*

Scientists sure know how to rationalise the irrational. 'Heart failure', I suppose, if we're going with layperson's terms. I make notes of how to describe this when I call Bee and my mum in a minute or so. I jot thoughts:

- *painless*
- *quick*
- *sudden*
- *there's nothing we could've done.*

I scroll onwards. The webpage lists symptoms: chest pain, coughing, fatigue, lightheadedness, palpitations, trouble breathing. He had been convinced it was long covid. I learn more, at that moment, about the ways a heart can break.

I research alcoholism. Social → Binge → Heavy → Dependency → Addiction → End-stage. The children of people with an alcohol use disorder face a twofold greater risk of developing one. It's useful to know the odds, what we're up against. I've already got his psoriasis.

After making the calls, I run up to the moors. *Natural.* Hands at my hips, I pause below a peace monument. I breathe deep, 1,300 feet up. *Natural?*

'If I keep going til that gate, he'll get better. To that tree, to that lamppost. If I put my right sock on before my left sock, right shoe before left shoe, then everything will be okay.'

As a child, my mind used to whisper such things. Still does, sometimes. These wish lists made about as much sense as everything else. I find them hard to shake. My dad acted as if nothing could break him. Since he broke, I'm prone to anticipating life shattering at any moment.

Running is where I do my clearest thinking. I see I need to look more carefully. I sit on my favourite rock above the tawny valley and study the glaring lime fields. 'Improved', authorities call them, like they call his death 'natural'. Improved and natural only by our declining standards.

My heart and headphones pump 'Reasons to Be Cheerful, Pt. 3'. It's just me and the sheep up here among these vast, barren hills that render life vivid and trivial. The moon's in the midday sky, full and glinting. A lone leaf crunches underfoot as I hurtle downhill, arms outstretched. I note to myself that I am free free free.

~

Here goes, Pt. 1. I drag screenshots, photos, notes onto blank pages on my laptop. I don't own a printer. Instead I attach the document, plus two of the interminable legal forms I have to fill in, to an email for our library to print. It tells me the file is too big, morphing into a monstrous, conspicuous Drive link. Oh god, they will not handle this.

I head into town and greet our librarian, harbouring a sheepish, one-line plan for how I might explain eleven pages of hostel room images, missing person appeals, messages, and prison notes if, or let's face it, *when*, she asks. She smiles and slides the two legal forms below the see-through screen.

I survey these sheets with a casual expression, then say without looking up, 'Ah, yep, just one more document I think.'

She opens my email. 'Nope. Two here, love.'

I direct her towards the Drive link and she clicks open the sordid PDF. The palaver is only just getting going. The file takes ten searing minutes to traipse across the Wi-Fi to the printer while she loads and scrolls each page, one by one by one by one.

'What neat handwriting you have,' she remarks, scanning my dad's rants across the weekly activity packs doled out by Cardiff Prison.

'It's not mine.' I pause. 'It's my dad's.' I hesitate again. 'For a writing project.'

She nods, still smiling, ish. At last, she surrenders the eleventh page (I get a printer a year later).

I buy a cork-board from the nearest charity shop. £2.50, bargain. Even comes with pins. At home, I fasten all this heart-related evidence onto what is fast joining the ranks of the world's bleakest pinboards. Look, I'm a visual person and it's my route to grasping his cause of death. The real reason, natural or otherwise.

Truth is, I had almost forgotten about the post-mortem. Expectation management, you see. My dad never explained himself, and who turns over a new leaf in death? *Inconclusive*, the interim certificate had said, and I assumed that this verdict would continue. That's not to say I didn't sometimes wonder why he had to die so young. Accepting the essence of mystery doesn't preclude mulling it over.

I know he didn't really leave us that night outside the VW dealership. He had come and gone for years, wandering a path that's hard to map. In theory, I last saw him on that lunch-break. Wednesday 13 February 2019, 1,048 days ante mortem. In reality, I could hardly see him in that garbling man I met. I can't pretend to fathom how he managed to disappear and reappear for so long.

An incoming call from Bee. I'm on the clock, but I pick up.

'It's happened again,' she says.

'Hello to you too. What's happened?'

'They dug up what Mum planted, primroses or something.'

'Oh.' I switch my phone to the other ear and refresh the podcast's Twitter feed.

'It's a *natural* burial meadow,' I sigh. 'I've told her like a hundred times she can't keep doing this.'

'I know, but you know what she's like.'

I retweet something about trees.

'I swear to god, they're gonna take her trowel and exhume him if she carries on.'

~

It's another bizarrely blue sky when I make my dad's death official at Calderdale Register Office. A lunchtime appointment. I retire him as a notary public, erasing details of how he had to leave after, even he admits, too many days spent drunk and disorderly. In his own words:

dishevelled
asleep at my desk
agitated
solitary
withdrawn

He deserves an acknowledgement of how he 'worked like a dog' to make our lives what they were, thanks to the soulless job that no doubt played a role in reshaping his heart (a working theory). He gave us everything, from laptops to trips to bank top-ups, the car, the house, the panic attacks, my Master's degree, my habit of fleeing, my readiness for loss and instability. And when we in turn gave him the silent treatment or anxious looks, he was angry at us, the traitors. I see it in his notes from the streets:

Winter 2020 – bewilderment + grief anger at Betrayal. I worked so hard to pay for those houses + the lifestyle they led (holidays in California + South Africa – stupidly expensive hotels). Gone from a blazing triumph to a complete failure so suddenly. Trauma upon trauma. I had just been good for one thing – making money.

Didn't he know I'd have handed it all back in exchange for the dad he used to be? I realise he never wanted to deny us. We had to have all that he hadn't had. As our tooth fairy, he always left £2 coins below our pillows. Well above the going rate. A decade on, he shot down my idea of budgeting when I began my degree. He'd have given us anything, anything but sobriety.

On his death certificate I amend the last known address, disguising the hostel behind a veneer of Welsh. I keep it together. The registrar would never know I feel bereft in this moment. On the drive home, I'm grateful for a red light to gather myself. I have a work call in twenty minutes.

That night, I switch off my lamp and head up the moors again in my mind. There's my old mate, the kestrel, beating his wings above the reservoir. Both here and there I inch towards him. He flies further away the closer I try to get, out towards the centre of the water, surrounded by warning signs about sudden death.

Why, how, what signs might I have missed? I need to know before I do any of my own parenting. It's among the main reasons I'm investigating. We all have to be pragmatic, head above surface, at a time when even facts are disputed.

so full of life

In mid-May, abruptly, my team is let go. I thought I was joining a call to discuss renewing my contract, but the podcast has been bought out. We're no longer needed, apparently. I am shocked, but I then recognise it as a blessing.

The next day I apply for a job and am invited to interviews. By early June I've accepted an offer and requested a September start date. This summer must prove to be anything but redundant. It's exactly what I need to make something of all these notes I've scribbled since my dad died five months ago.

I write for entire days at the kitchen table. I write in evenings and at weekends. Even while out, I'm never not writing. My head whirs with what I have to put down. I recall the chaos of my former life from a distance, here by my open back door. *Sophie's Memoirs* Pt. 2, but my dad is only with me in spirit this time. The garden hums with songs of robins, an acorn-gatherer's chatter, the sloping trickle of a stream.

This trickle soon dries up. It's blisteringly hot, even up north. I chew ice and we keep the blinds drawn. Ash flops onto our folded-up duvet and asks the weather app when it might rain. The trail into the woods behind our home is easy footing now. There's no longer the thrill of the once slippery plank, spanning where the once waterfall flattened into the once bronze brook.

'What's with all the brown water?' I wondered aloud when we first arrived in the valley. The internet clarified: peat, leaked from the moors. All around us now are harebells and bog cotton, house martins and swallows. This language was all Greek to me a year ago. Now I look and I see.

Ash and I walk along canal paths and through woodlands, IDing wildflowers in the cracks of drystone walls. Old mill chimneys jut from the luminous green canopies. We wander around Heptonstall on a hilltop nearby, always stopping by Sylvia Plath's grave. I am struck by the inscription: *Even amidst fierce flames the golden lotus can be planted.* It was chosen by her estranged husband, Ted Hughes, whose surname pilgrims regularly chisel off her headstone.

Out of curiosity, I pick up Hughes's *Collected Poems* from the library. On page 924 I meet one of Ovid's daughters, Mestra. We have things in common, Mestra and I. Her dad likewise mocked the gods and took it too far one day by felling a sacred grove with an ancient oak. This didn't sit well with its goddess, Ceres, who reacted with a curse. The more this Earth-Tearer ate, the worse his hunger got. Insatiable, he turned to bartering his own child, transactions that Mestra desperately swerved. None of his efforts were enough and eventually he consumed himself. I think of a line from one of my dad's notebooks:

He always seemed so full of life, laughing + joking + begging for scraps.

There are echoes, echoes everywhere. My dad drank like he was infinite, invincible. Overlooking all he already had, everyone he might have lived for.

~

A Radio 4 guest forecasts the onset of feral girl summer. Imperfection is in. At last, I'm on trend this season. I turn in my chair. Time to review my latest findings into our Ultimate Question, what it's all about, though I no longer have my dad here to discuss it with. It gets me wondering: why did his heart change shape?

You know by now, his was a complex death, full of scope for an original response. Instead, my outward approach is as clichéd as a school-kid's simile. First I opt for frivolity (getting blonde highlights in my hair) then I try for enlightenment (booking myself onto a Buddhist retreat in the South of France).

I decide to make a trip of it, my July search for enlightenment. I tie in visits to old friends in Düsseldorf and Paris. In Germany, I eat waffles and drink a pilsner on the bank of the Rhein. In France, I eat p.a.c.s and drink wine at a canal-side bistro. I laugh with these wonderful people who have known me for over a decade, who knew my dad. I travel between cities on pulsing trains, notebook in lap, staring at the blurred scenery. He is never far from my mind.

When I pull up at my destination, an hour from Bordeaux, I find it all garishly bright. There are vines everywhere. People look shiny and happy. It's not the rugged France of the north, the country I know, where villagers hung about at bus stops and scowled at us through the drizzle.

I share a taxi to the retreat and check in with one of the nuns. I pitch my tent as the sun sets, then sit upright in a plastic white chair under a ripening plum tree. In-breath, out-breath, I attempt present tense. It's a learning curve. I look at all those around me, yearning to know themselves and process stuff. This would be my dad's idea of hell.

A gong wakes us at 5 am each day. We get dressed in the dark and take minibuses to the hamlet where activities take place. Each morning there is a sitting meditation in a big hall. A day or two in, I'm asked if I could drive a minibus. Sure, why not, I reply. I forget that it will be quite unlike the electric car I drive at home. I lug myself into the left-sided driver's seat and quickly try to get the hang of the clutch, gearbox, headlights. I am clownishly bad. The passengers have to advise me how to turn on the engine. I get us there, eventually.

'Nowhere to go, nothing to do,' the room chants, monotone.

I soon realise my sense of urgency sets me apart. My mind flickers about on this thin meditation mat, dancing between past and future. I have everywhere to go and everything to do. Another gong rings out from time to time, calling on us all to drop still and silent. It's a bit like 11/11, but it's a reminder about living, not dying.

An open mic session is heavy going. I'm last to join and first to leave, slipping out of the side door and dodging a pile of Amazon boxes that smirk, mindfully. There's illicit coffee and sunshine to be sipped. Call it a salutation, if you will. Afternoon wafts in on a barely there breeze and the schedule directs me to a 'sharing'. We gather in a circle and a monk asks our aspirations. It's my turn.

'Well, I'm new to this scene,' I hedge, meeting a few people's eyes, 'So this feels weird. I guess my upbringing wasn't very, uh, communicative.'

The spotlight presses me. 'Thing is, autism ran through my grandad, dad, and brother, so yeah I'm really not kidding about the lack of comms expertise.'

I recall the task. 'Ah, my aspiration? Right, I suppose I want to live intentionally. Because like, I've seen what can happen if— if you don't.'

I bow, which, I've learned, is a spiritual over and out. I hitch a ride back to my campsite in a Volkswagen of nuns. I bump heads with one as I lunge ignobly into the backseat. I apologise. She doesn't respond. I ask the woman at the wheel whether she's been here before.

'Can we do silent driving,' she says by way of reply.

I nod and look out of the window. Fields of grapes tickle the village's pledge not to consume intoxicants. I fidget with my seatbelt silently, mindlessly, and suddenly register my three (three!) coffees today. I hope this won't push enlightenment out of reach.

The next morning I eat vegan ice cream at speed, clumsily. I'm late for a deep relaxation. A slab of dark chocolate cracks off and melts on my right sandal. I rub the smear as I flop down. We focus on body parts one by one. It's an exercise that plays the role of a mellow straitjacket to keep us here in the moment. The nun moves onto the heart with a remark on how it's been beating since we were tiny embryos. My brain conjures this line into a placard an anti-abortionist might wield. It's an unrelaxing avenue of thought, soon pursued by musings on what I'm really here for.

So, why did my dad's heart change shape?

A nun tells us that 'repeated actions become habits become personality becomes destiny.' But what's behind the repeated actions, I want to know. Did he choose, or was it chosen for him?

'Picture your father as a wounded boy,' a monk says in another guided meditation. I consider bolting, but I'm in the front row. I screw my eyes shut and give it a go. Besides, my dad did the groundwork for me among his notes from the HMP, the only time I saw any hint of guilt in him:

Dream of being a frightened boy holding on to a high mast of a ship in a ferocious sea.

Guilt – all-consuming – what have I done to my family? is it all my fault?

I get so angry with myself. They say be kind to yourself. I don't want to be kind to myself – I don't deserve it.

'*Ton père en paix,*' the monk whispers, again and again. 'Your father at peace.'

Next, he has us imagining our mother as a wounded girl, '*Ta mère libre.* Your mother free.'

My father at peace, my mother free, my father at peace, my mother free?

I can imagine the laugh my dad would have had at my week-long pilot in Buddhist practice. I asked him about religion once while he was shaving in that narrow bathroom's mirror. I watched from the airing cupboard as he shook his head. 'It's all fairy tales, baby girl.'

He toyed with it for the census nonetheless. A Jedi Knight here, a Jainist there.

'We Jainists don't kill animals,' he said. He was adamant that we must never hurt bugs, despite the fact that he ate fish like a gannet. I smile on remembering one of the nonsensical lines from his notebooks:

I think all farm animals should be hand-reared and privately educated.

It's my penultimate day in this shiny bit of France. A monk sets us homework to find the joy in suffering. I'm a dab hand at this, I think. I studiously try to pinpoint the most beautiful moment my dad and I ever shared. I sift the past. There are many contenders: splashing about in water, clambering up mountains, sprinting across finish lines, laughing at our silliness. For every dark time, there are hundreds of memories beaming with light.

I miss our valley, the birds, the stream of unceasing chatter. I dream of home, where there's somehow always a cat hair floating in my coffee. Four days left. The excitement of homegoing. I wonder if this is my answer to our Ultimate Question. I realise, belatedly, that my dad shared his conclusion in that poem he wrote for my 21st.

Across all the commotion of my dad's end of life, there are contradictions I can't distil. The liberty he must have tasted in submitting to addiction, the prison and release of it. I sit quietly in solitude, watching the twinkling sunshine bob on a lily-padded pond. Above me a buzzard circles slowly, soaring the warm currents. There are no clouds. Nothing is the same as it ever was.

~

Seven months later, I'm in Llandough hospital's canteen. It's dusk. I'm sipping machine-brewed hot chocolate when Bee and our mum come through the doors. They pull up chairs. Bee begins to shred my wooden stirrer. We make the smallest of talk. When we get up, my mum finds a penny. *Good luck*, we think but don't say.

'I bet it's from 1973,' she says confidently, handing the coin for me to check. She's not wearing her glasses. I don't ask why that year. I look and it's from 1984. I put it in my pocket without a word.

They head up briefly to West 2, Ward Room 21. I've just come down from there. It's Grandma, you see. She has suddenly become very ill. I took the train home as soon as I heard. I wrote loving things in a *pili-pala* card and watched Grandma read it earlier as I poured some sparkling grape juice, the closest I could get to her beloved Prosecco. We had a makeshift aperitif together. The nurse made her keep on her oxygen mask. 'See ya,' I smiled at her as I left.

Yes, it's different this time. There's a hospital, visitors, 'see ya'.

Different, too, because this has shocked me. I'm not prepared. Since visiting her, I know she's going to die and I sob in my hotel room in Cardiff city centre. I didn't know where else to stay. I order room service, a veggie curry and a glass of Prosecco in her honour, then turn on the TV. *Four Weddings and a Funeral* is on. I catch it early and watch until the end. Ash and I are getting married this summer. Grandma is supposed to be throwing us a party. She has already chosen her outfit.

I make a list of things I'm grateful for: that she could be at my graduation; that I could surprise her with a visit on her last birthday; that I could be at her Christmas party eight weeks ago; that I could get here in time to make her laugh today.

When I wake up, I swim in the hotel pool then take Danny on a spontaneous day-trip to Bath by train. I let him choose what we do. We eat pies and mash, then go on a tour up the abbey tower. We are 160 feet above the streets. The winding steps and low ceilings terrify me. I watch Danny like a hawk. If he has a fit— no, it doesn't bear thinking about. Meanwhile he's absolutely loving it, asking questions and giggling at the tour guide's jokes. We crawl behind the face of the clock and look at the hands of time ticking close up. I relax only once we're back at ground level. We go for hot chocolate and browse the shops. It's one of my favourite days I've ever spent with him.

The next morning, I walk through town to Bee's house in Canton. I detour for a takeaway coffee and hope the barista doesn't spot my swollen eyes. I cried again before check-out. I join a work call in Bee's kitchen, video off, and am half-watching a lightning talk when my phone buzzes. A text from my mum:

Thu 16 Mar 2023 10:23 AM

Grandma just died peacefully ... She is with Grandad and your father now.

I message my manager that I'm logging off. Bee comes into the room and I break down as I tell her the news. She holds me tight. This time she's composed and I'm crying. We've swapped roles.

'Ugh, she would go and die on Lloyd's birthday, wouldn't she?' Bee says.

We laugh then, and we laugh about the text, the idea of Grandma with our dad.

'At each other's throats, I bet,' we say.

I just can't get my head around it, how she could be gone. Just a week ago, she messaged:

Hi Sophie are you ok thinking of you today

My dad's birthday, it was. He'd have turned fifty-seven. I'm reminded how irreplaceable we are to those who love us.

~

In early June, Ash and I bring together all the people we love to Devon for our wedding. We're seeing the venue for the first time, here and now.

'Well, to be fair, I did FaceTime the hosts in autumn.' I shrug. 'Seemed legit.'

We make a long weekend of it and somehow have deep blue skies throughout. I can't help but think my dad had something to do with all this ludicrously good weather on days when it most matters. I did put in a sneaky request to him each time. I feel his presence as I step towards the aisle in the walled garden. Fresh air, trees, all you need. I know he'd agree.

In my speech I share something I read recently about a gentle rhythm of life, seizing moments of pleasure, eating well, resting well, cultivating friendships. I look at everyone's faces, their smiles and sparkling eyes. I could cry with happiness.

Echoes, echoes of the words I wrote aged five, sat beside my dad, on 25 April 1999. *I love my world.* And I do love my world, knowing how hard we have to hold onto it, how lucky we are to be here.

In Latin, *liber* means *book* and *free*. This story began in winter, remember? Sunset in the valley, still and chilly. I picture the pub, that crackling fire, how the landlady, Elva, must have sloshed my undrunk wine down the plug. I wrote then of *hirmynd*, long going. The fading of the dad who was with me once. I feel closer to him again since writing this. These pages have brought a freedom, *hirdod*, long coming. A homegoing.

I'll close for now at another beginning.

A month has gone by since our wedding. I'm typing these last lines in the windowsill of our new home on the Welsh border. An old farmhouse, an hour or so from Cardiff. We're starting a nature restoration project. Beyond our window are rolling meadows and sprawling oaks. Tonight there are peachy, peaceful skies. Ash spots an owl swooping and we scurry out for a better look. It's just us and the birds, or so I thought.

'See the beauty,' my dad sings into the soft air around us. I smile, taking it all in. I won't know it for a week or so, but my daughter has begun growing quietly inside me.

There's no unseeing the ugliness of some things my dad did in drunkenness. Still, I don't even need to look to feel his undying love for us. I can trace its shape, eyes closed. And, at the end of the day, when all's said and done, he was just a man, standing in front of a universe, asking what it's all about.

Acknowledgements

These are the people I'd like to thank, by order of appearance in my life:

My mother, who carried me into the world.
My father, who so lovingly shaped it into an oyster for me.
My grandparents, who enriched my early years with such distinct ways of seeing and being.
My brother Danny the champion, who blazed through life like a lightning strike – I hope you and Dad are having happy times together again.
My sister Bee, who is all the very best bits of what family can be in one miraculous human.
My friends on the street, who filled my childhood with giddy joy.
My friends since primary school, Li, Pip, and Milno, who are essentially siblings to me by now.
Meine Austauschpartnerin Lea, who is among the wisest and kindest people I know.
My friends from high school, especially in Form S, Welsh, and German, who made weekdays fun.
My Welsh teacher Lona Evans, who sparked my lifelong love of Cymru by whirling us around our nation and encouraging me to read and write beyond our curriculum.
My English teacher Jude Brigley, who first took me to Tŷ Newydd and revolutionised how I thought of exams: 'How lucky you all are! Enjoy!'
My headteacher Michael Griffiths, who imbued our state education with the arts – even taking the whole school to the opera!

My friends from university, Em, Turner, Han, Geeg, Eri, Izzy, and Mona, who rollercoastered with me into adulthood and have been the epitome of sisterhood ever since.

My everything, Ash, who means more to me than words could convey – we grew up together and we grow closer with every year that goes by.

My second family, Pam, Darryl, Barbara, Hayden, and Kate, who are the most loving, supportive in-laws I could have dreamt of.

My de facto brother-in-law, Lloyd, who gets us all so deeply it feels like he has been here forever.

My teammates from RPT and IWDA, who inevitably became friends for life.

My cats, Indi and Eva, who bring hilarity to daytimes and irreplaceable cosiness to evenings.

My anonymous reader from Faber Academy, whose How's My Driving? report made a real difference.

My agent, Philip Gwyn Jones, who guides me with profound wisdom and attentiveness.

My editor, Rebecca Parfitt, who brought this book into being and takes such a thoughtful approach both to me and to my words.

My publicist, Lynzie, who is the understated queen of all things marketing.

My neighbours and friends along the Welsh border, who welcomed us here with open arms.

My daughter, the absolute light of my life, who is forever reminding me of the infinite ways to see the beauty.

ABOUT HONNO

Honno Welsh Women's Press was set up in 1986 by a group of women who felt strongly that women in Wales needed wider opportunities to see their writing in print and to become involved in the publishing process. Our aim is to develop the writing talents of women in Wales, give them new and exciting opportunities to see their work published and often to give them their first 'break' as a writer.

Honno is registered as a community co-operative. Any profit that Honno makes is invested in the publishing programme. Women from Wales and around the world have expressed their support for Honno. Each supporter has a vote at the Annual General Meeting. For more information and to buy our publications, please visit our website www.honno.co.uk or email us on post@honno.co.uk.

Honno

D41, Hugh Owen Building,
Aberystwyth University,
Aberystwyth,
Ceredigion,
SY23 3DY.

We are very grateful for the support of all our Honno Friends.